The Ethics Of Belief:
A Bio-Historical Approach

Volume I: Theory

Kenneth Cauthen

CSS Publishing Company, Inc., Lima, Ohio

THE ETHICS OF BELIEF: A BIO-HISTORICAL APPROACH
VOLUME I

Copyright © 2001 by
CSS Publishing Company, Inc.
Lima, Ohio

All rights reserved. No part of this publication may be reproduced in any manner whatsoever without the prior permission of the publisher, except in the case of brief quotations embodied in critical articles and reviews. Inquiries should be addressed to: Permissions, CSS Publishing Company, Inc., P.O. Box 4503, Lima, Ohio 45802-4503.

Library of Congress Cataloging-in-Publication Data

Cauthen, Kenneth, 1930-
   The ethics of belief : a bio-historical approach / Kenneth Cauthen.
     p.   cm.
   Includes bibliographical references and index.
   Contents: v. 1. Theory — v. 2. Application.
   ISBN 0-7880-1873-6 (v. 1 : alk. paper) — ISBN 0-7880-1884-1 (v. 2 : alk. paper)
   1. Christian ethics. I. Title:
BJ1251 .C275   2001
241—dc21
                                                    2001037904
                                                                CIP

For more information about CSS Publishing Company resources, visit our website at www.csspub.com.

ISBN 0-7880-1873-6   PRINTED IN U.S.A.

To my grandchildren

in the hope that they may live in a world with more justice and love in it than the one my generation is leaving to them and that they may play a part in making it so.

Table Of Contents

Volume I

Preface To Volumes I And II		7
Chapter 1	On Doing Ethics	15
Chapter 2	What Is Truth — And Does It Matter?	49
Chapter 3	Telling It Like It Is — Can We? Reasoning With Rorty	77
Chapter 4	How Can We Acquire Moral Truth? Three Answers	107
Chapter 5	The Ethics Of Christian Belief: Theory	135
Chapter 6	The Ethics Of Christian Belief: Practice	167
Index Of Persons		205
Index Of Subjects		207

Preface To Volumes I and II

The present work is presented in two volumes. The division is basically between theory and application. Volume I deals with the nature of ethics as a form of philosophical and theological inquiry. I propose an approach which I call the ethics of belief. I also look into the sources of moral belief. Finally, I develop a theory of Christian ethics. I set forth what I think love and justice mean and imply within a biblical framework. Volume II takes up a variety of contemporary moral problems. I take forthright positions on a number of current issues about which American society is deeply divided and give the reasons for believing as I do. The two parts go together and form one unified whole. However, I have tried to present them in such a way that they can be read in independence of each other. Nevertheless, the theory presented in Volume I looks forward to its implications for policy and practice. The second volume presupposes the first part as its foundation. My hope is that readers will want to take them together. Yet those whose interests are primarily theoretical will find that the first section holds together by itself. Others who wish to get immediately to a discussion of specific issues without the encumbrances of theory will find that the second part can be read separately quite intelligibly.

A preface may serve a useful purpose if it provides a clue to the aim and perspective of the author. These two volumes are an example of ethics done on the boundary. I find myself on the border between church and world, theology and philosophy, revelation and reason, Bible and culture. I have a dual identity. I am both a believer in the church and a self in the world. On the edge between these two spheres I wrestle with issues of right and wrong, good and evil, duty and destiny. This makes for a certain complication in the way themes are dealt with. I function as both theologian and philosopher as I try to make sense of the moral life. I see no conflict between these two roles or between what I perceive to be true of morality from each vantage point. I try to show how and why I find this to be the case. Nevertheless, readers who expect to find a single-minded perspective written from the standpoint of philosophy or theology may find the movement between these two approaches disconcerting. I can only confess that on the border between church and world is where I find myself as I seek to discover what it means to be a responsible human being. I am a person with dual citizenship, and this vantage point on the boundary defines the approach to ethics in these volumes.

The first volume develops the ethics of belief. Simply put, communities and their members have convictions about right and wrong, good and evil. This is what ethics is about and where ethical inquiry should begin. I maintain that we should simply confess what we presently believe about morality, give the reasons why we believe as we do, recite the history that led to our beliefs, and leave it at that. This means we do not make any claims that our views are objectively true and universally valid. We have no way of knowing whether they are or not. We can only acknowledge where we stand and what we see from that location. We hold certain beliefs because we cannot deny them. We have no option but to witness to what we are compelled to believe. We cannot pronounce those who hold contrary views to be in error. We can only say that we believe them to be wrong. The details and implications of this view must be left to the fuller exposition found in the chapters that follow.

The ethics of belief is set within a context of relativism, skepticism, and pragmatism. All moral points of view are relative to the time and place of those who have them, whether they be communities or individuals. Truth claims in ethics can be developed and tested only by the means available to us at the given point in history where we find ourselves. That is the basic meaning of relativism. Relativism does not imply that one point of view is as good as the other. It would be difficult to find anyone who seriously believes that we cannot discriminate between better and worse morality. Nor does relativism mean that no outlook corresponds to reality. It only means we cannot be sure which one, if any, does. That is what I mean by skepticism. It is literally true that we walk by faith and not by sight. Finally, relativism does not mean that we cannot judge some moral beliefs to be wrong. We simply say they are wrong from our perspective and that we will act accordingly to oppose them in every appropriate way.

Relativism and skepticism lead to a pragmatism in which we seek a way of understanding things that best accounts for all the experiential evidence available to us and that is internally consistent. An outlook that meets these tests can be useful in guiding us and assisting us in coping with life. In my case the fundamental insights about morality that hold me in their grip have been provided by the Christian tradition. Central to this outlook is the love of God for us and the love of God and neighbor required of us. I believe this way of viewing the moral life is in fundamental harmony with what my reason and experience teach me. I see no dissonance between viewing morality as a self in the world and as a believer in the church as I stand on the boundary between these two forms of citizenship. I readily agree that my reason agrees with my faith because my faith provides the perspective within which I think about things. Then when I use reason to make an independent test, it is not surprising that it finds my religiously-based beliefs not only credible but compelling. In reverse fashion, nothing is admitted into my theology that reason tells me cannot be true. This merely means that my beliefs form one unified system.

I define my way of viewing ethics as a biological and historical approach. We begin as creatures of nature with a genetic inheritance that took billions of years of evolutionary development to produce. We come out of the womb as a biological organism with the inherent possibility of growing into an adult human being. We have a drive in us to actualize the potential of our natural endowment. I call this urge or desire *eros* — the hunger for what satisfies, for what is good and fulfilling. *Eros* is a multidimensional and variable energy that ranges from the sexual to the sublime, from the erotic to the aesthetic. At its highest levels it is the quest for the true, the good, and the beautiful. *Eros* is the love that unites us from birth to parents and forms a bond of community with them. It leads us into sexual unions that create families. It urges us beyond ourselves to develop friendships with others that extend the community of those who are loved. It is capable of indefinite enlargement into wider communities of mutual support and reciprocal service. We love those for whom we have sympathy and are willing to sacrifice. We love those whose good is a part of the good we seek for ourselves. Our natural urge to seek our good in community with others is the basis on which we may come to love them as we love ourselves.

Christian love (*agape*) is unconditional concern for others in which we regard their good equal to our own without regard for their merit. *Agape* is the perfection of *eros*, not its opposite. It is the extension of our biologically-based loves (*eros*) toward universal community so that no neighbor is excluded. It regards every human being as equal to the self in worth. *Agape* serves the neighbors' need without regard to the worthiness of the recipient or whether or not the other person responds with an answering love. When we identify our good with the good of our neighbor, when neighbor includes all other human beings, and when we love our neighbor unconditionally, *eros* has united with *agape* and become one with it. Ethical *agape* is identical with natural *eros* directed toward a universal community in which every human being is our neighbor who is loved unconditionally. In this boundless community no one is excluded from the common good sought by each for all and for all by each. This is ethics on the boundary also of *agape* and *eros*. *Agape* and *eros* are not opposites but apposites. Christian love (*agape*) is an historically-developed way of organizing the biologically-based energies of *eros* in the life of individuals and communities. Justice is the social expression of love in which we seek to determine what each and all are due under various circumstances.

The main ethical problem, then, is not that we love ourselves instead of others. Nearly everybody loves some other people from infancy onward, not perfectly but genuinely. The problem is that we love everyone imperfectly, and we draw limits and exclude some partially or totally from our sympathy and concern. We are morally immature. The moral task is to extend the natural *eros* that unites us initially to family and friends until no neighbor is excluded from the circle of those who are naturally loved. Our challenge is to develop and nurture loving persons who will spontaneously do what love requires. We need to learn to love better those we already love and to begin to love those whom we scarcely love or do not care for at all. There are, of course, individuals and groups that hate some other people and are cruel and violent toward them. All of us love imperfectly and exclude some from our active compassion. Not neglecting the fact that immoral persons exist to do evil to others deliberately, the main issue is that we are all morally immature to one degree or another. The crucial challenge is to learn to include those we now leave out and to love everybody better than we do.

The moral task is not to persuade our reluctant wills to take the neighbor's good into account when in fact we would prefer to seek our own selfish aims. Virtuous persons do virtuous deeds as a natural expression of their moral character. The challenge is to create and nurture virtuous people. A good tree brings forth good fruit. We are commanded to love our neighbor as we love ourselves. It is better to think of this not as an imperative that tells us what we ought to do but as an indicative that tells us what we will naturally and spontaneously do when we have become fully mature moral persons. What we do expresses what we are. The role of churches is to help create and nurture loving persons who will grow up into full personhood so they will naturally do what they ethically ought to do (Ephesians 4:11-16).

New Testament Christianity is incompatible with civilization. It assumes the imminent end of the age; worldly institutions are passing away and don't matter much (1 Corinthians 7:24-31). It makes absolute demands (Matthew 5) that are irreconcilable with life in a complex organized society in which moral ambiguities abound and only the roughest approximation to justice is possible. Our failure is not that we make the compromises necessary to live in a continuing society with defined roles and responsibilities, but that we make them far sooner than is necessary.

I conclude by making some suggestions as to how we can relate to others who agree and disagree with us as members of the same or of other communities. The basic point is that we should engage in conversation to explore our several points of view, to compare and contrast them, to defend our own, to persuade others to accept our point of view, and to form alliances with those who share a common commitment to accomplish ends we deem to be worthy of our joint efforts. What we should not do is get in a fight over who has the objective truth that is universally valid.

When the theory of Christian ethics has been developed in Volume I, I proceed in Volume II to look at some contemporary issues in the light of the ethics of love and justice. Love honors the intrinsic worth and promotes the well-being of the neighbor. Justice seeks to maximize freedom, equality, and the good life for all within the constraints that each of these aims puts on the others. The procedure is to begin with some contemporary situation and ask how it is illuminated by love and the quest for universal justice. I take some positions in ethics that are controversial and unpopular. I urge the decriminalization of prostitution and the eventual legalization of drugs such as cocaine and heroin. Marijuana should be decriminalized immediately. I call for a one-payer, Canadian-style health care system that provides universal coverage. I insist that we should not only overcome destitution and poverty but take measures that will reduce the massive inequalities of wealth and income in this country. I call for the legalization of physician-assisted death in certain extreme, desperate, and hopeless situations. I contend that abortion is a morally ambiguous problem that has no satisfactory solution other than the prevention of unwanted pregnancies. I oppose capital punishment, although I recognize that a strong argument in principle can be made in its favor. The unfairness of its current administration makes it totally unacceptable. I urge that we will fall into confusion unless we distinguish between the issue of church and state and that of religion and politics. I indicate how I think religious faith should be expressed in political action. I argue that the time has come to stop oppressing homosexual persons and to accept the moral legitimacy of responsible same-sex love.

In brief, this is what the ethics of belief done on the boundary is about. I am indebted to many others for most of the ideas that compel my agreement. There are too many to begin a list, lest others of equal importance be left out. However, there is no mistaking the fact that Alfred North Whitehead is my primary philosophical guide, while the Niebuhr brothers Reinhold and H. Richard have taught me most of what I know about Christian ethics. Putting it all together for myself is first of all a need I have to integrate and systematize my own thinking for practical purposes. The results are offered to others for whatever usefulness they may have in initiating a conversation about the moral life. Serious engagement in humility, openness, and reciprocal respect can explore agreements and disagreements as well as lead to possible mutual conversion. Our aim should be to assist each other in order that we may all be better equipped to think and act responsibly in ways that make the world a better place to live.

Kenneth Cauthen
Rochester, New York
September 15, 2001

Chapter 1

On Doing Ethics

> *If medical students enroll in an ethics course to determine if they should perform abortions, all they will learn after examining all theories is that some people believe such action to be justified and others do not. Ultimately, as before taking the course, the decision on how to act will lie in the medical student's personal value system. They will not resolve painful dilemmas with ethical theories, but rather with their own values acquired throughout his or her life.*[1]

Ethics as a form of intellectual inquiry does not provide answers to moral questions. People with beliefs about right and wrong do. Philosophers and theologians engaging in the formal discipline of ethics can develop principles of moral obligation. They can take positions regarding the grounding and justification of moral belief. They can take positions on specific moral questions. They can analyze, systematize, and classify theories of ethics into types and schools of thought and write histories of ethical thought. What they cannot do is tell us the certain truth of the matter. Ethicists can only report the conclusions they reach when doing ethics. Ethics as such has no rules, methods, sources, or ways to ground and justify ethical belief. Ethics as such does not provide right answers to questions about right and wrong. Ethics tells us only what those who engage in ethical inquiry think and believe about morality.[2]

People have moral beliefs and sometimes live in accordance with them, and sometimes they do not. They do some things because they believe they are right without necessary reference to consequences and do other things because they believe they will accomplish more good than alternative courses of action. In other words, they act for deontological and teleological reasons,[3] but most have never heard of those words and have little sophistication about ethical theory as it is practiced by the specialists. People act on the beliefs they have acquired over a lifetime. Philosophers and theologians become technical experts in the history, language, and methods of ethics as a formal discipline with its many schools of thought. But they are still people who, equipped with the tools of the trade, work out their own systems of thought and make pronouncements about good and evil. They incarnate their own thought into the formal schemes they adopt. Ethics, however, does not tell them what is virtuous, just, and good. People who do ethics specify that in the formal theories they appropriate or create as experts who know how to give precision and systematic expression to their judgments.

Ethics As Beliefs About Morality

Philosophers from the time of Plato and Aristotle have claimed that reason could discover ethical principles that are objectively true and authoritative for everyone.[4] They, of course, know that they stand in a particular historical location, but they typically assume that from where they are, they can rightly discern right from wrong as it is written in the nature of things. Christian thinkers likewise have assumed that inquiries based on divine revelation lead to the truth about morality.[5] While theologians acknowledge dependence on a specific history, the ethical outlook that results is usually held to be the standard for everybody everywhere. In other words, philosophers and theologians have typically held an objectivist view of ethics. This means they assumed that if you use the right methods, you can discern principles of conduct that reflect an objective order of reality and value. For most of my professional life I did ethics in this fashion. I no longer do. I do not believe there is a method, whether based on reason or revelation, by which principles of ethics can be formulated that can be known with certainty to be in correspondence with objective reality and hence universally valid.

I reject the objectivist approach in favor of the ethics of belief. The place to begin is with the moral beliefs of a community or an individual that arise out of a particular history. These convictions can be authenticated only by reference to the means of acquiring and testing truth available to a given community or person. Most Christian thinkers, of course, would agree with this. They look to the biblical witness for the source and norm of truth about our duty and destiny. So far, they will find much in my presentation to applaud. Some would insist that moral claims are to be tested only by their fidelity to that witness and not by any canons of human reason. Christian ethics, they maintain, need not and cannot be tested or contested by rational criteria. Here we differ. Moreover, many will be offended by my skepticism and relativism, especially if their confidence in divine revelation gives their moral convictions a foundation that guarantees their objective truth and universal validity. Other theologians would insist that reason can play a role in discovering and testing moral truth that is objectively true and universally valid, as long as its claims are subordinated to the criteria that certify Christian identity. The varieties of Christian belief cannot be encompassed by a few simple statements. Each community and each believer will have to find their own peculiar agreements and disagreements with what follows.

I do not reject the notion of an objective order of reality and value to which true statements correspond. I believe that we live in a value-impregnated environment that has a structure independent of us to which experience provides clues that reason can interpret in systems of belief.[6] But I do not believe we can know for sure whether our moral and religious beliefs correspond with reality. The usual procedure is for individual interpreters and religious communities to claim universality and objectivity for what they themselves believe. Am I far from the truth is saying that right and wrong for individuals and communities are identical with what they presently believe? I do not know of philosophers or theologians who maintain that a moral system other than their own is actually the true one. The bolder thinkers simply declare contrary beliefs to be in error. Those who have been infected with milder forms of relativism opt for a pluralism that maintains that while they may not have the whole of reality in their grasp, they have a valid perspective on it. Or they may hint that all of us may have bits of the truth but that they have the larger pieces, the more adequate view. The problem is that they cannot say with certainty just how accurate their perspective on the whole is or state exactly which pieces are true and which pieces are false. If they could, they would have no need to embrace relativism of any sort. They could just say plainly what was objectively true. Hence, they are precariously balanced between an absolutist objectivism and a thoroughgoing relativism that is too unstable to be of much good, apart from the comforting assurance it provides.

I am a skeptic and a relativist. I believe that all large-scale claims about the nature of things and the order of values rooted in objective reality are relative to the time and place of the interpreter (culture or individual) and that we can never know with certainty whether our beliefs correspond with the independently-existing order of things or not. After applying the rational tests of logical consistency and adequacy to evidence, I embrace a pragmatism that relies on satisfying workability in practice rather than objective certainty or rational confidence about theories of existence and value. I believe that it is literally true that we walk by faith and not by sight. This way of thinking about ethics can provide strong convictions and lead to actions that express them. It can generate and sustain moral passion and afford us as much courage in adversity as any alternative. We can assert as vigorously as we need to that views contrary to ours are wrong from our perspective and act accordingly. We can oppose with force practices that are so reprehensible that a milder response is inadequate. Ideally this orientation will combine passionate commitment to a vision with humility of outlook. We can debate with others about the grounds for knowing whether certain practices are right or wrong, while acknowledging that we have no way of knowing for sure which alternatives are in harmony with the objective order of reality and value that exists independently of our belief.

Relativists, of course, have been around since at least the time of the Sophist Protagoras.[7] He was promptly refuted by Plato, and relativists in every subsequent generation have been pounced on with equal vigor by the successors of Plato eager to establish the universality and objectivity of moral truth in utter confidence in their ability to do so, or at least with respect to their version of it. Yet relativism never stays dead. This might suggest that the relativists are on to something not vulnerable to objectivist attacks. We all recognize that on some occasions it might be appropriate, or at least prudent, to live by the maxim implied in the saying, "When in Rome, do as the Romans do." Usually, however, we are more willing to consent to this advice with regard to manners, etiquette, and protocol in which a breach of social custom might cause unnecessary offense to others and embarrassment to us but would not constitute a violation of moral law. When fundamental issues of morality are at stake, the universalists and objectivists, not the relativists, have defined the mainstream of thought.

An element of relativism is sometimes acknowledged when speaking of an erroneous view thought to reflect assumptions dependent on the culture that produced it. Aristotle, for example, is condemned for believing that slavery is dictated by natural law. He was blinded by assumptions common to his age. Some Christian commentators have noted that the unliberated views of Karl Barth on women reflect what we might expect from a Swiss man of his generation. They do not typically go on to say that their own more egalitarian views reflect their own cultural locale. They are just true. Usually the views taken to be normative are thought to be exempt from the relativity that authors find in others. We are not generally advised by the ethicist who is currently speaking to beware of the possibility that what he or she is capable of believing is circumscribed by the same kind of social, cultural, and historical factors that limit the unenlightened. I want to insist that all moral outlooks are shaped by the culture in which they occur, not just the erroneous ones.

Not only does the thinker live in a particular culture at some given historical moment, but she/he is defined by a whole set of individual particularities — gender, class, race, education, nationality, religion, life history, and on and on. I have read a large number of books on ethics, philosophy, and theology over the last fifty years. I do not recall that any two of them took exactly the same position on every point. Like snowflakes and fingerprints, the variety of views on moral truth appears before us in magnificent splendor. It is a matter of integrity that you must disagree with everybody else on some point. Viewing the moral order from a particular temporal-social location, of course, does not preclude wide areas of agreement with other persons or even other cultures. Nor does it mean that the claims that result are not true. It just complicates the problem of knowing which ones are. The difficulty is that no one can examine the objective moral order from some vantage point above and beyond all particular places, a spot that provides an unfiltered view of things as they are.

The central quest of the traditional approach is to discern the universal norms that define personal virtue and social justice. So each generation of thinkers looks at the systems of ethics produced by history, compares and contrasts them with one another, makes a choice among them, or proceeds to add one more scheme to the tradition. The systems are generally taken as they are as self-defining, stand-alone productions of thought to be assessed by norms that are regarded as universal and objective that presumably all competent persons who are correctly instructed could come to be in possession of. Christians, of course, measure moral claims by the standards thought to be decisive for that tradition; but the virtues, duties, and ideals of life thus generated and approved are thought to be obligatory not merely for Christians but to define God's will for all people.

I am not maintaining that we are totally bound to the moral wisdom we have inherited and that it is therefore impossible in any significant way to transcend our historical relativity. This underestimates the power of human creativity and unduly limits the capacity of the imagination to produce fresh visions of ideal possibilities to which we can aspire in quest of more just and more fulfilling ways of living. Cultural consciousness changes, and the moral beliefs held by societies and their philosophers and theologians change over time. Each new stage views its own insights as having overcome the errors of the past. Slavery is out of fashion these days, but a century and a half ago it was defended by learned scholars and pious clergy.

I do not propose to abandon entirely the use of principles. They have an essential place in the total enterprise. However, I do wish to set this approach into the larger context in which thinking about right and wrong occurs. So doing will illuminate both the legitimacy and limits of searching for principles that point us toward the good and away from the evil. The main point can be simply stated. The ethical point of view of a community is relative to time and place. The outlook of an individual within that community is conditioned by her/his unique personal identity, social location, and life history. I state no unqualified law or rigid determinism and assert no absolute relativity in these matters. We are not dealing with physics here but with the strange, wonderful, and baffling chemistry of the human spirit. We must recognize the astounding potentialities of free, rational beings with capacities for creatively transcending conditions and imagining new ideal possibilities for the human adventure. But to neglect the finitude and historicity of ethicists and the resulting relativity of their thought is to miss an essential ingredient in the formulation of moral beliefs.

This raises a problem. How can we declare all ethical systems to be relative to time, place, and culture and yet speak with authority about where previous generations went wrong? How can we declare that anything is just plain right, then, now, and always for everybody? I believe there is a way to do this, but it involves a frank recognition of relativity even while aspiring to universality. I reject the assumption that reason can produce ethical beliefs that are independent of the history and culture of the reasoner who formulates them in such a way as to merit the status of universal, objective moral truth. As an alternative I propose to set forth a view that begins with particular communities who have a history and a set of informing traditions. Human imagination over time creates myths of origin, beliefs about people, nature, and ultimate reality. Each culture evolves a code of ethics, and a collection of stories, symbols, and rituals to celebrate and perpetuate a framework of meaning and purpose that enables its members to understand and cope with the world and achieve a good life. Numerous are those who claim to have escaped from Plato's Cave to look at pure truth, goodness, and beauty. The problem is that when they return to the darkened interior, they give conflicting reports of what they found in the light of the sun. The problem is knowing who the impostors are.

The most fruitful approach for communities and individuals who engage in conversation with each other is to recite the history that led to their particular system of values. Each may give the reasons for the beliefs held and be open to new insights, while rejecting in the other what is unconvincing. However, each must forego the privilege of claiming absolute validity for her/his own perspective or of pronouncing others to be simply in error. It is permissible only to assert that the other is wrong when viewed from the preferred stance. This is better than for the contending parties to argue for and against value systems as abstracted products of thought that, although generated in history and culture, can be discussed independently of them. The usual assumption is that history and culture are like a ladder that gets us to the top of the house. Once we are there, we can dispense with the ladder, and argue for the universality and objectivity of our beliefs and values, while trying to demonstrate that the alternatives produced by other histories, cultures, or individuals are just wrong. Most moral disputes take place among contending parties who all claim to be speaking the truth, the whole truth, and nothing but the truth. Each claims universality and objectivity for its own outlook. Believing that one's own outlook is in harmony with the order of values ingredient within reality itself may give one confidence and produce good feelings. It may provide reassurance in the presence of contrary views. But claiming universality and objectivity for a point of view helps us not at all to determine what is actually right or wrong in a given situation. It contributes nothing to the process of determining the actual content of belief. I contend that this approach is not a useful way of thinking, has not worked, and is not convincing when confronted with the overpowering evidence of the relativity of moral points of view. One outlook might in fact be universally and objectively true (correspond with reality), but we have no way of demonstrating that to be the case. Hence, I am led toward a pragmatism that (1) tests beliefs by the best we know up to now and (2) by their power in practice to make the world intelligible and to achieve a fulfilling life. Put otherwise, we affirm what we cannot deny and seek for better beliefs when our presently operating scheme fails to meet the aforementioned criteria.

What Ethics Cannot Do

As the medical students who want to know if abortion is wrong find out, ethics as an intellectual discipline will not and cannot give them the answer. It will give them many answers, arguments for and against, ways to analyze and clarify the problem, and a lot more, but it will not as such give the solution that is purely and simply correct. More precisely, philosophers cannot discern the moral structure of reality as practitioners of pure thought who transcend their temporal and social location. They cannot examine the moral universe with immaculate eyes, attending solely to reality itself as it reveals itself with perfect clarity unfiltered by any prior assumptions or bias rooted in cultural background or personal history and experience. It is not indisputable or self-evident that pure reason demands one and only one set of moral beliefs such that contrary views would be irrational or wrong. No methods or procedures can be devised that will lead us to the truth about good and evil by merely using them correctly. Reasoning is done by historically-located reasoners. Moral beliefs arise in communities with a history and with a culture. Reasoning about ethics always takes place within this context. Judgments made by individual ethicists within a culture reflect their life experiences, training, and personal reflections. No technique of reason can avoid this cultural conditioning in a way that opens insight into objective truth as it is in itself. It is not possible to leap over our inherited and developed assumptions into universal validity and to be sure that we have done so.

Let us grant that if we stay at a high level of generality and with purely formal definitions, wide areas of agreement may be possible. Not many would argue with a truism like the first principle of natural law in Thomistic thought that urges us to "do good and avoid evil."[8] That would seem to be obvious once we have committed ourselves to thinking about morality in a moral way. That is what being moral means. But what specifically is good and what is evil? Specifications at the level of particulars bring culture and individual interpretation into play. Justice can be defined formally as "giving to everyone what is due." Is this more than a tautology, since we are likely to think that justice defined as denying what one is due is self-contradictory? But what are specific persons due in given circumstances?

Justice can be defined as always involving impartiality among equals. As Aristotle put it, "Now justice is recognized universally as some sort of equality ... justice involves an assignment of things to persons ... equals are entitled to equal things."[9] Surely most of us would agree that equals should be treated equally if we are to honor justice. Thus far pure moral rationality might take us. But who is equal and in what respects? Moves toward specifying who is equal to whom and in what particulars lead us into relative judgments made by communities and persons immersed in history. Aristotle did not think that slaves and masters were equal. We might concur that mutuality, reciprocity, impartiality, and equality are essential elements in discerning what fair treatment requires. Nevertheless, even if we are able to get agreement on some formal factors like this, we are still a long way from producing a complete ethical theory containing concrete judgments about right and justice on particular matters.

The Golden Rule of Jesus might take us a little farther along (Matthew 7:12). If we treat other people as we would want them to deal with us, we are likely to act in a highly moral way, since we presumably want people to do good to us and deal with us justly. By identifying self with other and other with self, we can usually get good guidance, given the assumption that we value ourselves, our needs, and our interests. Yet the maxim of the Golden Rule is reciprocity. So an act of adultery when all relevant parties approve, including the spouses of the participants, would presumably meet the standard. Hence, it would appear that we need to make an assumption that the Golden Rule itself does not contain. The full rule would state that we should do unto others as we would want them to do unto us if we were totally virtuous and fully wise about what best promotes human well-being, justice, and goodness, all things considered. Those who think God has defined faithful monogamous marriage as the norm would not accept mutual agreement as the sole or sufficient rule of morality in this case. Neither would those who believe that adultery is usually harmful, even if accepted by all parties. In any case, more needs to be said than is contained in the Rule itself. That once again introduces the role of a historically-located interpreter with a point of view.

Likewise, much can be said in favor of Immanuel Kant's Categorical Imperative stated as the formal principle that we should act in such a way that the maxim of our action can be rationally legislated as a universal principle. Put otherwise, it bids us treat humanity, whether in our own person or another, as an end and never simply as a means. Finally, it urges that in acting, our wills should function as a universal lawgiver, so that what is valid for us as an autonomous rational agent is valid for everyone else as well.[10] Surely there is merit in taking all persons into account as ends when we act as moral legislator for the whole human community. Yet these formal injunctions are void of specific content. For example, is it ever right to lie? Kant thought it was not. Different interpreters making use of these same principles may reason otherwise, some allowing a lie and others forbidding it in specific instances. Here too the moral judgments of communities and individuals arising in history and culture are required to complete the system of moral beliefs. Moreover, critics delight in providing examples in which an act that is clearly wrong would be approved or listing acts that are clearly right that would be forbidden by Kant's proposal.[11]

Reinhold Niebuhr maintained that mutual love is the highest form of rational morality.[12] We might agree that this is the highest form of ethics reason can produce, but mutual love is not the norm toward which rationality inevitably or universally leads. Moreover, love as a general principle does not tell us what love requires in concrete instances. Love has been thought to be compatible with all sorts of things most of us today would deem reprehensible — persecution of heretics, slavery, segregation, subordination of women, and so on. As a Christian, Niebuhr goes on to make *agape* or sacrificial love a higher demand that is, at some points, not justifiable on a rational basis in that it may require the unjust sacrifice of self in service of the neighbor. The *agape* ethic requires grounding in faith in God that does not allow what happens in this life to be the final point of reference. Hence, mutual love is not necessarily or inevitably where reason leads; and even if it did, it is insufficient according to Niebuhr, reasoning as he does from within a particular religious community.

Some thinkers have attempted to find a purely rational concept of justice by creating a procedure that is as free from as many contaminating value assumptions as the situation will allow. Two devices are especially noteworthy. Roderick Firth and others have imagined an Ideal Observer (IO) or Judge.[13] Suppose that an impartial, relevantly informed, rational, benevolent being sets out to construct the framework of a just and good society composed of human beings just like us. What principles of justice and morality would such a being prefer whose intent was to benefit all with prejudice toward none? Obviously, certain advantages result from being perfectly good and having complete knowledge of the facts. Beyond that, however, someone has to ascertain what judgments the IO will actually make on particulars. Any interpreter is just one more historically-conditioned individual with a particular outlook. Inevitably, a society constructed in this fashion will be created in the image of the author. For example, would a society created by Aristotle in the guise of the IO have slavery in it? Apparently it would, although Aristotle himself makes impartiality between equals an essential element in justice. It is simply that slaves and masters are not equals in the requisite fashion, since some are by nature fit to rule others while others are only qualified to be ruled.

Another notable effort to achieve objectivity and universal validity by a relatively value-free procedure is the Original Position (OP) hypothesis of John Rawls.[14] He is representative of those who try to provide a basis for social ethics in the absence of an agreed upon idea of the good. It is widely held in modern times that the good cannot be rationally defined but is a matter of individual and social preference. Hence, a way must be found for individuals who hold widely varying concepts of the good to form a society in which all willingly participate. Rawls has offered one of the most discussed procedures for dealing with moral pluralism in which individual choice is the fundamental point of reference. If a group of people wanted to construct a just society *ab initio*, what principles would they establish? Rawls begins by asking under what conditions would self-interested people neutral about their neighbors be willing to live and call them fair. The assumption is that they make their social contract in the OP behind a "veil of ignorance" to assure impartiality. The parties will have the general knowledge about people and society needed for their work. They will not know particular facts about themselves, their position in society, their native talents, their psychological propensities, their conception of the good life, or the generation to which they will belong. They will be ignorant of the specifics of their own society, its level of economic and cultural advance, and so on, although a condition of moderate scarcity is postulated. The aim is to decide what would be fair rules of procedure designed to secure the cooperation of all.

Put briefly, these stipulations lead, Rawls thinks, to two fundamental principles of justice: (1) equal liberty and rights for all, and (2) the equal sharing of all social goods except where inequalities will benefit all. Much that is commendable can be found here. Many Christian thinkers think that Rawls comes out pretty close to where a contemporary interpretation of New Testament ethics takes us. It is a monumental intellectual achievement. Yet it produces an egalitarian bias on selfish grounds. Justice as fairness is concerned with those who have less not because, as Christians would have it, we ought to love our neighbors as ourselves and therefore serve the needs of all with a bias toward the poor and outcasts. On the contrary, in Rawls' view the contracting parties realize that they might end up at the bottom of society. Thus they opt for a society that would be most beneficial to them if the worst came to pass. Hence, looking out for the needy is self-protective in this scheme. Hence, while many would find a wide range of harmony between Rawls and Christian conceptions of justice, it is a happenstance rather than a congruity of fundamental principles. If they could be guaranteed that they would not find themselves at the lower end of the social scale, the contracting individuals would not choose an equal sharing of social goods but would prefer an arrangement in which they might have more. This is not what Christians are taught about sharing with the needy.

John Rawls has by no means convinced everyone of his principles of justice. The criticisms are too extensive and complex to review here.[15] The critics complain either that this is not the way to go about defining justice, and/or they insist that Rawls has not come up with the right principles. The idea that people can define justice in complete ignorance of the conceptions of good and right they hold strikes some as odd. Some think that he has produced the framework of a society based on consent that leads to judgments of prudence that are not necessarily just. Others think that for the sake of equality he is willing to violate individual liberties and rights. Some condemn him for neglecting merit. All the critics think they, not Rawls, know what right reason about justice really requires. Is one party or the other deficient in rationality, or do these differences reflect something peculiar to the interpreters not necessarily demanded by universal reason as such abstracted from history, culture, and individuality?

Moreover, empirical judgments about particular subjects inevitably enter in when we get down to specifics. For example, he has been accused of underestimating the extent to which some people at least are willing to take chances, prepared to risk loss in order to get a better deal rather than opt for the best of the worst that might happen. Rawls thinks that the capacities essential to earning merit are mostly a product of genes and social upbringing and not an individual achievement worthy of reward. To what extent is that correct? Somebody has to make a judgment about that, and not everyone will agree.

The Ideal Observer and the Original Position methods have the advantage of making sure everyone is treated equally and impartially, but this is not enough to produce a system of morals that is valid, universal, and objective in a way that commands the consent of all rational interpreters. At a more fundamental level his colleague at Harvard, Robert Nozick, thinks Rawls' social contract procedure does not produce just principles at all.[16] He thinks all "end state" views that specify some required outcome are deficient. He offers instead an "historical entitlement" view. Nozick begins with autonomous individuals with inherent rights to engage in voluntary interactions and exchanges in order to pursue their interests (whether their interests be altruistic or egoistic). His core conviction is that justice honors voluntary arrangements, transactions, and exchanges. Outcomes that are produced by interactions freely agreed to are by definition just. People are entitled to what they have justly acquired or transacted for. Hence, three principles arise: just acquisition, just transfer, and rectification of unjust acquisition and transfer. Hence, while Nozick would allow whatever inequalities were produced by just procedures,[17] Rawls would allow no inequalities that were not beneficial to all, and would permit government action to carry out the principle. Both agree with the liberal tradition in recent Western thought that provides all with equal liberty. Can reason decide between Rawls and Nozick or offer a third alternative that is actually the right one? No, only reasoners can make those judgments, and they are certain to be contradicted by equally competent thinkers. And how can it be established as objectively right that individuals are the supreme legislators rather than having some central authority allotting roles, rights, and rewards to individuals on behalf of the community as a whole?

Another example of the attempt to derive a set of ethical reason by purely rational means is provided by the influential work of Alan Gewirth.[18] He argues that morality is not based on personal preference or social conventions but on the rational grounds given in the analysis of human action. People act on purposes they regard as good. The necessary conditions of acting purposefully are freedom and well-being. From this Gewirth derives the principle that all other people must refrain from eliminating or interfering with my freedom and well-being, since it is a necessary condition for my action as a human being. This is a right that I can claim for myself that others must honor. But since individuals have such rights by being human beings, it follows that all other human beings have identical and equal rights for the same reason. Here again the principles of equality and impartiality come into play in a fashion that it is difficult to argue with. What applies to one person must rationally apply to all. Everyone who wants to be avoid self-contradiction must act on the following precept: "Act in accord with the generic rights of your recipients as well as of yourself."[19] Gewirth calls this the Principle of Generic Consistency (PGC). "The PGC is the supreme principle of morality because its interpersonal requirements, derived from the generic features of action, cannot be rationally evaded by any agent."[20]

Once we get that far into the analysis, Gewirth may be right. Nevertheless, is there anything necessary or self-evident about beginning where Gewirth does to get to that point? Even if we grant the reasonableness of beginning by asking about essential features of being human, already in answering the question Gewirth brings something of himself and his own convictions into the picture. The more he goes on to specify particular human rights and what they imply for the organization of society, the more his point of view becomes his own in a way that is not shared by other equally reasonable thinkers. In the end he has a point of view that is his and that can be contrasted with other thinkers who have their own particular approaches that, while reasonable, are not self-evident or necessary.

A still different approach to justice refers to another of the grand traditions in European thought. Rawls, Nozick, and Gewirth present deontological theories in the tradition of John Locke and Immanuel Kant. Franklin Gamwell develops a teleological theory by identifying with the more ancient tradition of Thomas Aquinas by setting ethics within the context of a comprehensive vision of reality with the help of Whiteheadian metaphysics.[21] Eschewing the modern consensus that the good cannot be rationally defined, Gamwell sets out to do just that by defining the good human society after the pattern of divine purpose. He refutes the typical objections to ethics devoted to maximizing the good. It is commonly held that teleological ethics strictly adhered to is prepared to trample the rights of individuals for the sake of achieving total social good. Moreover, the good cannot be maximized by our actions alone since, in the absence of settled rules, we cannot know or depend on what others will do. Gamwell meets both objections by allowing that binding rules can be established that are themselves both necessitated by and grounded in the imperative of maximizing the good. The background conditions or formative principles create rules, duties, and social practices that must be followed regardless of consequences. Among these is the necessity of a democratic polity that assures equal participation by all in the processes that create the rules by which all must live. A just society will maximize the general conditions available to all that lead to enriching of life in all its varied dimensions. Contrary to a widespread assumption in modern thought, Gamwell not only argues that the good can be defined rationally but also sets ethics in a religious context in which the reality and purpose of God are essential to the theory and practice of ethics — thus protesting in a double fashion against the prevailing fashions in secular moral philosophy. At the most fundamental level, he thinks that deontology is simply wrong, although he attempts to incorporate what is valid in that approach into his own system. Some things must not be done regardless of consequences. The result is a reasonable way to think about justice but hardly what reason necessarily requires, as his opponents are quick to point out.

The point of this brief tour is to make two points: (1) Some widely accepted high-level generalities and purely formal principles may be useful, even essential, but they do not provide us with much specificity. For that we must turn to particular cultures and individuals whose judgments are relative to time and place. (2) No procedure, not that of the Ideal Observer, the Original Position, or any other, allegedly free of adulterating initial value assumptions, can itself produce just principles that are self-evidently true or that will command universal assent. Particularities peculiar to interpreters inevitably enter. Nozick refutes Rawls, and Gamwell rebuts both. Other philosophers reject them all in one or more particulars. Hence, there is no unanimity on the principles of morality, at least in detail, and if there were, universal assent would be no guarantee of objective truth.[22] Nor are differences among cultures and philosophers a refutation of the objectivity and universality of moral truth. Reason is always somebody's reason. Reason produces specific judgments that reflect the historical, cultural, and individual background of the reasoner. These judgments are not necessarily required by some universal rationality. This becomes more evident when we move from abstract truisms and formal principles of impartiality, equality, mutuality, and reciprocity to more complete systems of morality and social justice provided by John Rawls, Robert Nozick, Alan Gewirth, Franklin Gamwell, and others. They differ from one another not because one or the other is deficient in rationality but because their total orientation to life — influenced by their life history, training, individual reflection, and personal value system — leads them to diverse conclusions.

Rawls, Nozick, Gewirth, and Gamwell do, of course, recognize that they stand in a particular community of interpretation. They consciously identify their location within strands of the larger European-American tradition. However, if I understand them, the claim of all is that while the stance of each is particular and subjectively authored, their conclusions are intended to be objectively true and universally valid. Moreover, they are prepared to argue for them as correct on rational grounds. They are valid for all, whether anyone recognizes it or not. None claims infallibility or sets forth absolute claims beyond criticism. Nevertheless, I do not find in them the kind of thoroughgoing relativism that I am defending.

To sum up, ethical inquiry cannot produce moral judgments that are indisputably true to which all rational persons must give consent or forfeit rationality. Ethics cannot be an autonomous inquiry whose only requirement is the ability to reason about humanity and the human situation. In particular, the approach to ethics that purports to set forth moral norms that are universally valid and objectively true is subject to two limitations. (1) Pure thought can come up with some high-level generalities and some formal rules that may produce wide agreement, if not unanimity, in the immediate culture in which they are set forth. But alone they offer no specificity on particular issues of right and wrong. All judgments on specifics are authorized by communities and persons with a past and a set of experiences. (2) When this approach goes beyond generalities and formalities to spell out concrete principles of justice and individual morality, the results bear the distinct mark of the time and place of the community or individual who created them. Of all the moral perspectives on ethics from Epicurus and Socrates to Rawls and Rorty, have any two of them agreed in every respect? Many of them differ in fundamental considerations. Utilitarians (teleologists) and deontologists refute each other daily. That should tell us something about the view of ethics as a rational discipline that can produce right answers to moral questions. While much agreement can be found in the religions and philosophies of the world, each comes to these agreed upon conclusions based upon an astonishing variety of assumptions reflective of a particular history and culture.

Cultures create belief systems and moral standards to organize their communal life in light of what they come to believe is true about human existence and its promise of good living. They develop norms, goals, duties, and laws. They create symbols to express their way of life and rituals to celebrate it. They bring up their children to live by the established codes of conduct and institute ways to punish deviants, and so on. It is there we are to look for moral beliefs and values. Philosophers and theologians are members of some such community at a particular time in history. Philosophy as a discipline cannot sufficiently transcend the historical and cultural location of philosophers to produce ethical norms that simply correspond to the nature of things. Or at least we cannot be sure that any culture or thinker has done so. The moral order is not open to our direct inspection so that we can compare it with the thought that claims to replicate it. Moral norms are available to us through reflection upon experience. Moral beliefs cannot be validated except in some interpretive scheme thus derived. This fact defines what ethics as a rational or theological discipline can do and not do.

What Ethics Can Do

Ethics is usefully understood as critical and creative reflection upon the moral traditions and practices of communities. Its point of orientation is the history of some particular society that has produced the variety and unity of moral belief that is actually present. It is within this context that the philosopher begins to think about what is right and good, the ends of life, and the virtues, duties, rights, and responsibilities that define life lived in accordance with the highest ideals. The intent may be to discover what is binding on all people and places past, present, and future, but what can be done, in fact, is to discern as best one can what is most worthy of belief from a particular vantage point. For philosophers in the Western world, this will mean thinking within the context of the heritage whose main line runs, with many tributaries, from ancient Israel and Greece through medieval Europe and into the modern world. Christian ethics will have as its initial subject matter the moral tradition of the Bible with a peculiar focus on the ethical implications of the life, ministry, teachings, and proper interpretation of Jesus. Philosophers and theologians recognize, of course, that they stand within a particular tradition, but most of them do not see in this fact any impediment that prevents them from seeing what is universally true as measured by the objective order itself.

Ethics understood as reflection upon moral traditions and practice will have three tasks:

A. Analysis

Ethics can describe and interpret a given moral tradition or particular individual outlook. For the individual philosopher this means identifying the particular trajectory of thought within which he or she intends to work or modify — Platonic, Aristotelian, Thomistic, utilitarian, Kantian, Chinese, and so on. A Christian ethicist will indicate the branch of the many-sided movement that provides the starting point — Orthodox, Roman Catholic, Protestant, or whatever. The underlying presuppositions that authorize that initial location or heritage or point of view can be uncovered and elucidated. A thorough interpretation would include an investigation of the history that produced it, seeking in the process for clues that explain its form and content. Ethicists frequently do this in varying degrees of depth and detail as a matter of course by way of setting forth the background and context for their own constructive efforts. Within this larger framework particular practices can be examined to show how they fit into the religious, philosophical, and cultural traditions in which they occur, either to exemplify or perhaps to contradict some of its features. So far the effort is not to judge but simply to understand.

B. Assessment

Most immediately assessment involves evaluating a particular practice in the light of the norms of a tradition or a particular articulated individual perspective. Is abortion ever permissible? If so, under what conditions? A culture or a community, however, may be internally diverse and contain a variety of traditions and practices. Part of the task of ethics is to evaluate the many strands within the larger historical and cultural background in terms of which of them most authentically represents what is central to its core assumptions. In the nineteenth century the controversy over slavery centered around whether the enforced servitude of Africans was in keeping with the fundamental values of the Republic. Abolitionists argued that the fundamental values of liberty and equality demanded the end of slavery. Natural law and Scripture were also claimed by both sides as favorable to their cause. Likewise, the Bible, natural law, and the founding documents of the country were brought into play to support or reject the right of women to vote. Recently Christian feminists agonized over whether a usable past could be found in the Bible and Western history. Many appealed to neglected strands within Scripture more favorable to the equality of the sexes. Moral philosophers in every generation evaluate the legacy from the past. They identify with those traditions and schools of thought that support their own rendering of the ends and duties of human beings. They reject the alleged errors of the past that may be presently held by the less enlightened. This leads into the final task of ethics.

C. Revision

If nothing can be found in the moral legacy congenial to what the interpreter believes to be normative, a new vision must be promulgated. Usually, however, philosophers, theologians, and leaders of movements appeal to something found within the past but that has been neglected or misinterpreted. Much liberation theology of the last generation sought to recover the dissenting voices of marginalized or repressed communities. The controversy over same-sex love threatens to split churches today. Each side appeals to the cultural, philosophical, and theological past to buttress its point of view. If favorable passages of Scripture are available, they are quoted as authoritative, while disagreeable portions of Scripture are ignored or explained away. A final resort of liberals when chapter and verse favor the opposition is to locate a vital core of truth and to find in it a mandate for responsible homosexual love. Everybody, of course, claims Jesus, whatever the issue or cause. The contending parties are notoriously skillful in performing exegetical and hermeneutical miracles to ensure Scriptural authority for their own positions. The same Word of God is claimed as the authority for contrary positions. I have concluded that the Bible is for the most part a mirror in which all find a reflection of what they presently believe. I do not imply that Christians develop views independently of Scripture and then look for interpretative methods and texts to buttress them. Nor am I claiming that they are wrong in finding biblical warrant for them. It is simply that in the interaction between text and interpreter a moment of resolution occurs in which an identity emerges between what the interpreter personally believes and what the Scriptures are believed to teach when functioning as the Word of God for today. No dishonesty is involved. Nevertheless, when other Christians draw contrary conclusions, the explanation lies in the interpreter since all are reading the same Bible.

In the constant reinterpretation of received traditions old patterns of belief die and are replaced by emerging ones. No one today would be taken seriously who wanted to deny the vote to women or to justify the enslavement of Africans. Moral consciousness evolves. A century from now the condemnation of responsible same-sex love will seem as quaint, repugnant, and silly as the arguments for slavery and the denial of the vote to women seem today. Yet a century and a half ago philosophers and theologians were applauded when they argued that Scripture, natural law, common sense, and the good of society justified the ownership of some human beings by others and the restriction of women to hearth and home. The morality of sexual relations has changed profoundly in this country in the last half-century. What was once thought to be scandalous, e.g., couples living together before marriage, is now commonplace and evokes little attention.

In short, the ethical task is to carry on the conversation with the past, either to confirm its insights or to call for abandonment of its errors and the adoption of better ways of thinking and living. That is, as a matter of fact, mostly what philosophers and theologians do. Hence, the three tasks I have outlined do not constitute a novel proposal but a description of what actually goes on. What I complain about is that although they admit their historical location, most theologians and philosophers in effect play "At last we've got it." Seldom do they admit that their own point of view is as relative to time and place as the ones they reject. I claim that it is even if we all agree that some present conclusion is superior and, as far as we can tell, the ideal that we must live by from now on. Let me emphasize, however, that although ethicists cannot transcend their time and place altogether, they can creatively reinterpret it. We should not put prior limits on the power of the imagination to create new visions of a just and good society that ennoble the human condition. But the starting point is some particular set of traditions and practices that have a history that requires reformation.

Nevertheless, we observe a Lone Ranger individualism in which everybody has to have his/her own system and argue it against others. Frequently, this goes on in scholarly circles within the larger culture but relatively isolated from it. Scholars become an insulated community who talk mainly to one another, although a few emerge now and then to serve as public intellectuals who serve the large community. Reinhold Niebuhr in a past generation and Cornell West in the present bring the resources of a learned intellect dedicated to justice into the general conversation.

Implicit in what has been said is a distinction that needs to be made explicit. I refer to the difference between the history of a community with a moral tradition and the history of thought articulated in the elite intellectual traditions of the culture. The latter is part of the former, but they are not identical and sometimes have little to do with each other. The articulation and interpretation of moral belief, of course, goes on throughout the culture with varying degrees of sophistication and subtlety and with much, little, or no reference to or knowledge of the Aristotles, Kants, Lockes, Niebuhrs, and Gamwells of the world. Ordinary people every day do some things in order to achieve good consequences and some things just because they are right, whatever the results. In so doing, they have no consciousness that they are exhibiting teleological and deontological forms of moral behavior. There is a history of changing moral consciousness in which the high intellectual tradition is not the only or even the most important influence. Sometimes the rethinking of moral standards follows or is an accommodation to the changes in outlook among majorities of citizens.[23] The relationship between the history of the world and the history of philosophy and theology is complex. Neither a materialism that sees ideologies and values as the product of more fundamental socio-economic processes and class interests nor an idealism that thinks that ideas rule the world is adequate. Ideas arise in a historical-cultural context of material conditions, and both reflect and generate changes in the culture. Formal philosophical and theological thought is not identical with or the sole source of the moral traditions of a community and of changes within it. Nor is it a mere rationalization by thought of material interests and social aims of the classes they represent, although it may be. An analysis of how and why the moral consciousness of cultures and communities evolves is beyond the scope of this essay and the competence of the essayist.

Philosophers and theologians should see their primary task as the analysis, assessment, and revision of the moral traditions and practices of the people. Instead philosophers write their books mostly for each other. The result is that schools of thought come and go in the universities with little influence on the actual traditions and practices of the masses of people. I am not ruling out the efforts of individual philosophers to set forth their own version of moral truth. This is a perfectly legitimate thing to do. I am one of the proud practitioners of the art. All I am criticizing is the claim or implication that the content of their construal is what reason as such demands. My suggestion is that they simply say, "This is the best I know up to now." Likewise, Christian theologians can serve a useful purpose by sharing the results of their study and reflection with the larger community of believers. I merely suggest they ought to admit that they are offering their version of the matter and not what Christian ethics as such requires, or, heaven forbid, what God's opinion is.

Conclusion

It would seem obvious that people, whether trained philosophers and theologians or not, are the creators of moral beliefs. The grand tradition in Western thought has held something different from what I mean to imply by this statement. Plato, Aristotle, Aquinas, Kant, and contemporaries like Rawls, Nozick, Gewirth, and Gamwell are not of the opinion that they are only stating their beliefs. They claim to be setting forth moral principles that are objectively true. They see themselves as setting forth truths of reason potentially open to all rational agents who are free from bias and fully informed. It seems obvious to me, however, that what they offer us is their personal convictions about all the issues they take up. Augustine, Aquinas, John Calvin, Karl Barth, Emil Brunner, Stanley Hauerwas, H. Richard and Reinhold Niebuhr, and numerous others we could mention all stand within the Christian tradition. They all purport to be setting forth the moral outlook of the Christian community. Nevertheless, the imprint of their individual convictions is unmistakably evident, along with what they have in common as members of particular Christian communities. Evident also are the assumptions of the century and culture in which they were born. All of these philosophers and theologians illustrate the relativity I have set forth and defended. That all statements of philosophical and theological ethics are fundamentally dependent on the social location and personal history of the interpreters is to me unmistakable. Ethicists can justify their beliefs only by using the assumptions, categories, and modes of thinking available and convincing to each one. I have made that observation the fundamental orienting insight of the ethics of belief. Simply put, communities and their members have beliefs about right and wrong. Practically, this is what we deal with in the everyday world. How are we to relate to those whose convictions differ from ours? To debate about whose beliefs are right, true, correct, or reflect some objective moral order is futile and a waste of time. It gets us nowhere. The argument should be abandoned so that we may concentrate on what is beneficial in a practical sense.

Pragmatically, two kinds are activities are worthwhile. An internal and an external aspect may be defined. Internal relates to what communities and individuals do for and among themselves, while external has to do with their relations to other communities and individuals.

Internally: Communities and their members take positions on particular moral issues. They declare some practices right, others wrong, some complex and ambiguous, and so on. They can elaborate the foundations of their belief systems, decide how their principles are to be tested and justified, trace their history, and do whatever else they want to with them in terms of analysis, assessment, and so on. It adds nothing to what they think should be done or not done in a moral sense to claim that their convictions are true, i.e., in harmony with the ultimate nature of things, correspond with reality, embody the will of God, emulate the law of nature, or whatever. Most, however, in one way or the other will do just that or at least imply it. It is certainly appropriate for interpreters to indicate by using these or other terms how they deem their beliefs to be grounded or validated. Each community and individual can witness to their own moral faith in the public arena and contend that their views ought to be adopted by all as the standard of right and wrong.

In the last analysis each community or individual will carry on internal criticism by its own methods in any way it chooses. Nevertheless, my own suggestion for this activity would be threefold:

a. testing for consistency and accuracy in deriving special moral judgments from professed norms and underlying foundations of moral knowledge,
b. measuring the outlook by its actual consequences in experience for people and animals, and, finally,
c. revising the entire outlook encompassing both norms and their implication as a result of a. or b. above or as the outcome of rethinking the whole perspective on the basis of acquired new insights or further reflection, especially when weaknesses come to light or anomalies emerge.

Externally: Since all societies and individuals live in a world in which others have moral convictions contrary to their own or derive them from different sources, we need some realistic way to deal with them. I propose that two ways of relating are fitting:

A. **The first is conversation.** We and others can present our own views in the most favorable light, elucidate the reasons for holding them, narrate the history out of which they come, and whatever else the listener desires to hear. This should be done as a confession of convictions held to be worthy of belief. Vigorous debate about the merit of competing outlooks is by no means ruled out as long as each is presenting the content of belief and the basis for believing some things and rejecting others. Wherever possible dialogue should be conducted in an atmosphere of mutual respect, even when the views that are presented are regarded by the hearer as abhorrent. However, some moral positions may be so loathsome that this is impossible. No one should be expected to hear with appreciation what is regarded as contemptible. In these unfortunate circumstances the best course may be simply to break off conversation in favor of whatever forms of opposition in practice may be appropriate or unavoidable.

Three aims of conversation may be noted:
1. *The primary aim of conversation is to locate agreement and disagreement.* This relates both to particular moral issues and to questions of basic ethical theory: sources, norms, assessment, and so on.

2. *The second is mutual critique.* This involves three steps.
    a. Each can make an *internal* criticism of the opponent's outlook. This involves judgments about whether it is consistent or accurate in deriving specific moral views from its own professed norms and foundational principles.
    b. Each can make an *external* criticism of the other. This refers to an evaluation from the speaker's own point of view. A general critique of the theoretical structures and foundations can be elaborated, if it is acknowledged that it is made not from a God's-eye vantage point but from the standpoint of one's own patterns of beliefs. It also involves judgments about the weaknesses of a competing outlook in terms of its consequences in real life for people and other living beings. Has the actual practice of this moral outlook when tried been helpful or hurtful to people, or would it likely be if the proposals were actually enacted in real life?
    c. Each can make a *comparative analysis* of the opposing belief systems in the effort to show why one's own is preferred both in terms of its theoretical formulations and practical consequences in experience for living beings.
3. *The third purpose of conversation is conversion.* We are usually open to change when we are persuaded that our own outlook is beset with fatal weaknesses in the presence of a more inviting alternative. Hence, each party will want to demonstrate the weaknesses in the other and the merits of one's own. The effort to bring another around to one's own point of view involves all three of the activities listed under critique: internal criticism, external criticism, and comparative evaluation. Here, however, the aim is to change the other not merely to point out inadequacies. Of course, people will engage each other as they choose and not according to any formula laid down in advance by me or anyone else. Here Richard Rorty is surely right that no limits exist except conversational ones. This means that all parties can say anything they please or argue on any

basis or for anything they want to as long as others will let them. There are no rules for dialogue other than the ones we make and can get others to agree to. The "ideal speech" conditions laid down by Jürgen Habermas are nice but not always realistic. They may be honored more in the breach than in the observance. The problem is getting parties in conversation to agree to them and observe them in practice.

B. **The second form of interaction with others is to form alliances.** We will want to join with others who agree with us and contend against those who hold contrary positions. In so doing we will employ every suitable resource and engage in every legitimate practice that is effective. This might include forming organizations, seeking legislation, and a variety of other efforts. The aim is to explain, defend, enact, and otherwise foster adoption and practice of moral views believed to be important for human well-being. In extreme cases this may include the use of force to combat beliefs and ways of living that are so destructive that no other form of opposition would be fitting or effective.

What is not profitably done is to argue about which outlook best represents the objective moral order or corresponds to reality. This is nearly always useless, a waste of time. Each community or individual can deal with what is believed to be the objective moral order only in terms of its own internal standards for acquiring and testing moral truth. Interperspectival debate about truth and reality usually gets us nowhere and can without loss of anything important be abandoned. In short, to put it bluntly, I am suggesting that in conversation with each other we forget about truth and reality. They can be discussed only in terms of our differing beliefs about them. We have no way to determine whose views are true to reality except by using our own measuring devices. We have no way to be sure they are accurate. Uninterpreted truth and reality are not available so that we can test our interpretations by them. We should instead concentrate on getting agreement with others where possible and opposing them when necessary. The same procedures I would use to get someone to agree with me are the same ones I would use to prove that I have the truth that corresponds with reality.

So where does this leave us? In most respects we will be where we have always been. We live in a world filled with many disputes about what is right and good. These outlooks differ in their fundamental assumptions, the foundations of belief, the norms of right and wrong, ways of testing and revising positions, and so on. A great deal of agreement will also be present. Most often we find overlapping in terms of background assumptions, methods of discerning right from wrong, norms, goals, definition of duty, categories of virtue, and the like. Americans, whatever their religious or philosophical outlook, will have a great deal in common as citizens who share a common historical and cultural heritage. Defining where one perspective begins and another ends may be difficult. Saying precisely what constitutes a distinctive perspective may be even harder. Practically, it does not matter much. When people disagree, they will argue about the issue in question whether they share much or little in common with their opponents. Catholics and Protestants will agree at many points as Christians but approach some moral problems quite differently. Persons within the same or similar communities will be able to discuss and debate within a common framework and yet disagree about what is right and wrong in particular cases. Disputes within a given community will obviously take a different form in some respects from those that take place across a divide marked by different assumptions and ways of reasoning about duty, virtue, and the proper ends of life. Whether differing in fundamental postulates or having many in common, the contending parties lay out the reasons why they think they are right and why they believe the opposing parties are wrong. Usually no one is convinced by the arguments against them. Sometimes people do change their minds either by confronting arguments they cannot answer, coming to see things in a different light, discovering they had been wrong in their facts or in their interpretation of a situation, and the like. Disputants may even convert others to their point of view by the power of their reasoning or interpretation. Frequently change occurs when people discover in experience that their theory has destructive consequences in real life. The closer to home it comes, the more effective the transformation. Alliances are made by groups and individuals who share a common outlook on a particular issue, and sometimes they seek legislation to give the force of law to their moral claims.

All of the above are justified by the ethics of belief. The only thing that is different on the premises I have laid out is that we will quit claiming that our views of right and wrong correspond with reality, reflect the objective moral order, incorporate the will of God, represent correctly what the Bible requires, what Jesus would do or have us do, or whatever other designation one would care to add to the list. We can say what we believe, but we cannot say that our views are objectively true. On the basis of the ethics of belief we will give witness to what we cannot deny, affirm what we are compelled to in the light of the best we know from all sources and based on what experience teaches us about what happens in real life when certain theories and practices prevail. When we have done all we can to give the best reasons for believing as we do and rejecting the alternatives, we will leave it at that. We will not argue about whose views are really true, right, and good as judged by the objective moral order. We cannot say what the objective moral order requires. We can only say what we believe it requires. No way exists to bridge the gap between belief and knowledge in matters of morality. But beyond this theoretical claim is the practical fact that to argue about who is right is a waste of time, a vain, ineffectual, fruitless, worthless enterprise. It gets us nowhere. We should just stop it. Except for that reservation, all else remains as before.

In the next chapter, I will define more precisely the kind of relativism I affirm and make a defense of it.

Endnotes

1. Brian Everill, Department of Neurology, Yale University School of Medicine, in *The Scientist* 10[17]:12, Sept. 2, 1996.

2. I would also argue that science as a form of intellectual inquiry does not provide answers to scientific question; scientists do. The differences between science and ethics have to do with subject matter and methodology. Science employs methods of developing and testing hypotheses that allow for more precision of statement and greater capacity for refutation in the quest for

superior adequacy. More agreement is possible because science is limited to what can be known and justified by its methods. It gains its precision by restricting its subject matter to what its methods can investigate and its pronouncements to what these techniques can test. It has nothing to say, for example, about right and wrong, the meaning of life, and the reality of God. Progress toward greater adequacy is more easily achieved than in ethics as measured by agreement. In the end, however, scientific truth is what the scientific community presently believes.

3. Teleological ethics judges acts solely by their consequences, while deontology denies that consequences are all that matter and specifies some other way of defining right conduct, which may or may not include consequences as one consideration.

4. Two brief but useful introductions to the Western tradition of moral philosophy are James Rachels, *The Elements of Moral Philosophy*, 2nd ed. (New York: McGraw-Hill, 1993), and William K. Frankena, *Ethics*, 2nd ed. (Englewood Cliffs: Prentice-Hall, 1973).

5. See J. Phillip Wogaman, *Christian Ethics: A Historical Introduction* (Louisville: Westminster Press, 1993), Jeffrey Siker, *Scripture and Ethics: Twentieth-Century Portraits* (New York: Oxford University Press, 1996), and two books by Edward L. Long, Jr., *A Survey of Christian Ethics* (New York: Oxford University Press, 1982), and *A Survey of Recent Christian Ethics* (New York: Oxford University Press, 1982).

6. My reasons for believing this are rooted in a whole network of assumptions about reality and its ultimate Ground. This outlook has been set forth in a number of books such as *Science, Secularization and God* (Nashville: Abingdon Press, 1969); *Process Ethics* (Lewiston: Edwin Mellen Press, 1984); *The Passion for Equality* (Totowa, NJ: Rowman & Littlefield, 1987); *Theological Biology* (Lewiston, NY: Edwin Mellen Press, 1991) and *Toward a New Modernism* (Lanham, MD: University Press of America, 1997). Alas, all of them prior to 1990 illustrate the approach to ethics that I now criticize, and not even in the last two is my present state of enlightenment much in evidence in terms of the alternative I propose here.

7. One of the earliest statements of relativism comes from the Sophist Protagoras, as quoted by Plato, "The way things appear to me, in that way they exist for me; and the way things appears to you, in that way they exist for you" (*Theaetetus*).

8. ST I.II.94.2

9. Aristotle, *Politics* (Totowa, NJ: Everyman's Library, 1959), 86.

10. Immanuel Kant, *Foundations of the Metaphysics of Morals*, 1785 (Indianapolis: Bobbs-Merrill, 1959), and *Critique of Practical Reason*, 1788 (Cambridge: Cambridge University Press, 1997).

11. Cf., e.g., Henry E. Allison, "The whole issue of the categorical imperative is extremely controversial, however, and there are a large number of interpretations and objections in the literature. The basic problem is that the test seems to yield both false positives such as 'I shall smother infants who keep me awake at night by crying,' which is clearly immoral but does not seem to be ruled out by the test, and false negatives such as 'I shall play tennis on Sunday mornings when courts are available since everyone else is in church,' which seems both to fail the test and to be morally permissible. Although there have been many attempts to deal with these problems, it is not clear that any has been entirely satisfactory." "Kant's Transcendental Idealism" (New Haven: Yale University Press, 1983). Found on the Internet at: http://www.xrefer.com/entry.jsp?xrefid=552499

12. Reinhold Niebuhr, *An Interpretation of Christian Ethics* (New York: Harper & Brothers, 1935); *The Nature and Destiny of Man* (New York: Charles Scribner's Sons, 1949), II, 68-97, 244-86; and *Faith and History* (New York: Charles Scribner's Sons, 1949), 171-95.

13. Roderick Firth, "Ethical Absolutism and the Ideal Observer," in *Philosophy and Phenomenal Research*, Vol. 12, 1952.

14. John Rawls, *A Theory of Justice* (Cambridge: Harvard University Press, 1971).

15. One of the most cogent of recent critiques is Michael Sandel, *Liberalism and the Limits of Justice*, 2nd ed. (Cambridge: Cambridge University Press, 1998).

16. Robert Nozick, *Anarchy, State and Utopia* (New York: Basic Books, 1974). For a discussion of Nozick and Rawls within the context of a scheme that illuminates the basic differences between them, see my *The Passion for Equality* (Totowa, NJ: Rowman & Littlefield, 1987), 63-98.

17. More precisely, Nozick would not allow the state to take coercive action to reduce inequalities that result from just transactions. However, if individuals want to take voluntary steps to reduce inequalities by giving their wealth to the poor, that is fine.

18. Alan Gewirth, *The Community of Rights* (Chicago: The University of Chicago Press, 1996), and *Reason and Morality* (Chicago: The University of Chicago Press, 1978).

19. Alan Gewirth, "The Basis and Content of Human Rights" in *The Philosophy of Human Rights*, ed. by Morton E. Winston (Belmont: Wadsworth, 1989), 190.

20. *Ibid.*

21. Franklin I. Gamwell, *The Divine Good: Modern Moral Theory and the Necessity of God* (Dallas: Southern Methodist University Press, 1996).

22. Unless, of course, one defines truth as what an ideal community of rational inquirers would ultimately agree to (Peirce, Frankena).

23. Around 1980 I was interviewing a couple prior to performing their wedding ceremony. The woman announced that they had been living together for a couple of years. Upon reflection I was startled by two facts: how casually she told me this and how casually I received it. I could not imagine this disclosure being made in these circumstances in this relaxed manner to a Baptist minister in 1950. The change had not come about because the churches had done an about-face on the issue of fornication. Rather changes in cultural attitudes and practices had brought about an accommodation in the churches, often not publically acknowledged in its official doctrines, which usually maintained the ancient insistence on abstinence before marriage. Although some of its liberal theologians had taken a more permissive stance in books and seminary classes, the acceptance of what previously had been regarded as sinful was not indicative of the influence of liberal church intellectuals on the mass of believers but rather the result of changes in the culture of which church members were a significant part.

Chapter 2

What Is Truth — And Does It Matter?

A lot of debate takes place among philosophers today about the nature of truth. Alas, it is a morass of arcane jargon, technical analysis, precise definitions, and subtle distinctions in which competing theories slay each other right and left. Most of them mercifully vanish rapidly from the scene. Even the more prominent among them disappear after their fifteen minutes of epistemological fame, leaving only the major efforts to live in the history books.[1] While impressive as examples of mental acumen, intellectual agility, and logical skill, the products of these high-level exercises about which theory of truth is most adequate have little or no practical value. They help us not one bit in the routines of daily existence or in making decisions about ultimate matters of meaning, morality, and religion, not to mention their uselessness for generating wisdom in the penultimate realms of economics, politics, social policy, and culture. Is there a God? Does life have meaning and purpose? What is the supreme good human beings ought to seek? Should assisted suicide be legally permitted? All the debates ever conducted on the correspondence theory of truth versus its competitors stacked on each other never produced a solution to a single one of these questions or to many other subjects of importance, however interesting or entertaining they may be as intellectual pursuits as such.

What Matters And What Doesn't

The more important question, then, is not which among rival theories of truth is true but whether any practical consequences follow from believing one theory of truth rather than another. The thesis to be explored in this chapter is that while beliefs about reality and morality matter a lot, i.e., have practical consequences, beliefs about these beliefs matter only a little or not at all.[2] To be precise, I am suggesting that beliefs about reality and morality have practical consequences to the extent that people actually live by what they believe to be true and right or at least affirm that they ought to. We do not always live in accordance with our beliefs, but frequently we do. In the sense, then, that beliefs about reality and morality exert a strong gravitational pull toward living them out in experience, they have practical consequences. Again, to be precise, I am suggesting that beliefs about beliefs do not have necessary or inevitable consequences for the way we actually live. That they may have practical consequences for some particular persons or communities is an empirical matter and cannot be predicted in advance.

My particular concern is whether relativism, which is a belief about beliefs, is an adequate or workable foundation for ethics. Does relativism prevent us from discerning and affirming those principles most productive of justice and happiness for all? Can it sustain moral passion, courage, and commitment to live by the highest and best we know? Those who abhor relativism maintain that valid moral judgments mirror the objective structure of reality. Right and wrong are grounded in natural law or the will of God or some other pattern in the very nature of things. Otherwise all sorts of dire consequences follow. Not all criticisms assume the same definition or apply to every type of relativism. Some of the typical alleged defects can be listed. If moral claims reflect time and place rather than grasp universal truths, ethics rests on insecure foundations. If moral standards are nothing more than a collection of disparate opinions, they cannot have a binding or necessary claim on our allegiance. If moral judgments are merely subjective preferences or expressions of feeling, no appeal can be made to anything beyond that. Objective judgments about right and wrong are undercut. Meaningful debates about morality are impossible since there is no standard beyond the opinion of the disputants to serve as a basis for judgment. If moral values are relative to a particular person or group and not universal principles grounded in reality itself, no basis exists for calling people to a higher standard than the one they now have. Hope for moral progress is undermined. In fact, the very concept of progress is rendered meaningless. Unless moral values are anchored to reality, mirror something present in the nature of things, we cannot say that some moral views are inferior to others. Two contrary views could be equally valid, since valid only means that somebody prefers it. Worst of all, relativism ultimately is the equivalent of saying that might makes right since those who have effective influence or the power of coercion determine standards of behavior, beyond which no legitimate appeal can be made. While these criticisms may be valid against some versions of relativism, they completely miss the mark with respect to the form of relativism I espouse.

What Is Relativism?

It cannot be assumed that relativism means the same thing to everyone. In fact, a variety of definitions can be found in current usage, not all of which are compatible. Hence, communication and argument require clarification of the term and its alternatives. Three major types of views about the status of moral beliefs can be noted. I will define my outlook in relation to the other two. I intend to defend only my own brand of relativism.

A. Objectivism

True moral beliefs are objectively and universally valid. They may be justified by reason or by appeal to divine revelation. They are not subjective creations but discoveries of something independent of the minds that discover them. They are found not made, discovered not created. They are authentic whether anyone believes them or not. Moral reality is what it is whether anyone knows what it is or not in the same sense that the law of gravitation was in operation before the law thereunto appertaining was formulated by human beings. Some objectivists say that valid moral judgments are those that will be sustained by all right thinking people eventually if not now. Reasons can be given for a correct moral judgment that will convince all open-minded, fully-informed persons who take a moral point of view. Our present beliefs may be wrong, but further thought and insight may lead to better knowledge. Some moral beliefs are right and true, i.e., put us in touch with reality. Contrary beliefs are wrong and false, i.e., they misrepresent the way things really are. Some beliefs are so obvious that we are justified in saying that they are true, e.g., torturing babies for the fun of it is wrong. About others we may be unsure, but we can be certain that there is a truth objective to us. We can pronounce rival views wrong in accordance with the certainty with which we hold them. With regard to at least some moral questions, relativism can be overcome or transcended. Reason and/or divine revelation can unite us with what is the case in the nature of things. Two points, then, are essential to this position: (1) an objective moral order exists, and (2) on some crucial moral issues we can have reliable or even certain knowledge, eventually if not now, about what the objective order obligates us to do.

B. Objective Relativism

An order of truth, meaning, and value is real and objective to us. More precisely, those who hold this view believe this to be the case. Nevertheless, all actual systems of belief are relative to time and place and can only be established and tested by methods and standards internal to each outlook. We can never be sure that our assumptions, methods, and conclusions capture reality. No supreme court exists to adjudicate disputes among rival perspectives. Any such court offers no transcendent or absolute insight but only one more relative interpretation. The intention is to describe and represent the objective order of things in our theories and practices, but certainty about truth claims in the realms of morality, religion, and philosophy insofar as these involve high-level claims about the structure of things in themselves eludes us. Reality is available to us only in some version of it that is dependent on the perspective of the interpreter and exists among others likewise relative to their creators. We cannot definitively pronounce others wrong if we mean that their beliefs do not correspond to reality. We can say we believe they are wrong, give reasons for so believing, and act accordingly depending on the importance of the issue. Objective relativism, then, is objectivist about reality but relativist with respect to our knowledge of that reality.

C. Subjective Relativism

Moral beliefs are expressive of the dogmas, customs, convictions, beliefs, mores, preferences, feelings, or attitudes of some group or individual — and nothing more than that. They do not mirror an objective order of reality and have no validity outside the minds of those who profess them. They are made not found, created not discovered. There is no objective order of morality that can be used to judge among contrary outlooks. Moral standards vary from one culture to another, and no universal, absolute, culture-transcending standards can be employed to grade them according to their degree of truthfulness. Whether moral beliefs correspond to patterns within the nature of things independent of minds is not a proper question. The moral beliefs people profess and act upon have their origin and validity solely within the framework of their creators and advocates. We can express and act upon our own beliefs, preferences, values, and feelings in whatever ways we choose to, including opposing contrary views. We cannot, however, pronounce alternative ways of believing wrong or inferior to ours if wrong means contrary to universal, objective truth or something other than merely being different from ours.

To summarize, objectivists are objectivists with regard both to reality and at least some moral convictions. Objective relativists are objectivists with respect to reality but relativists with respect to our knowledge. Subjective relativists are objectivists with regard neither to reality nor to our knowledge. Many of the objections to relativism apply mainly to this last form of it.

This way of distinguishing between these major types of belief about moral beliefs is mine. Obviously, various subtypes and overlapping may exist. Others will want to revise them and perhaps come up with a more accurate rendering of the actual views held by our contemporaries. All I claim is that these three types point in general to alternatives that in some approximate versions are or could be held, with whatever modifications the authors would care to make. They are in a sense "ideal types" that may have a heuristic value even when not totally accurate with respect to every particular outlook that falls roughly within a given category.

Objective Relativism

Two issues need to be distinguished. (1) The first is whether an objective order of reality, meaning, and morality exists in independence of our beliefs about them. (2) The second is whether we can have reliable or certain knowledge of this objective order. The first question has to do with reality, while the second deals with our knowledge of reality. Important dividing lines between points of view turn on this distinction. I am an objectivist on the first question but a relativist on the second one. My objectivism, however, can only be justified internally, i.e., in terms of the whole sets of beliefs I have about reality. It is in this sense that I am a relativist. To put it differently, I am a skeptic. I do not deny the objectivity of moral standards. I affirm merely that we cannot be sure that there are objective standards. Nor can we be certain what they are. We can only assert what is compelling to us using the best methods of inquiry available at any given time, but all methods and conclusions are justifiable only within a particular point of view. Relativism for me, then, means that we can discover and test moral truth only by making use of the language and the resources available to us in our time and place. This does not preclude the possibility that these truth-finding, truth-testing procedures may actually put us in touch with objective reality. We are, however, left with the question of knowing for sure whether and when they do or not. We cannot be certain on the big issues of life, morality, religion, and death whether reality has been captured or accurately represented in our categories or whether we are mistaking a subjective conviction invulnerable against doubt for objective truth.

I have no doubt that torturing babies is objectively wrong. If morality has any meaning at all, if right and wrong have anything to do with what is good or bad for human beings, it must be the case that gratuitous torture of the innocent is wicked. This confidence, however, guarantees nothing. The crucial issue is that I passionately hold this belief. The remaining question of importance is whether I am willing to act appropriately to prevent the torture of babies in real life. My metaethical views are irrelevant both to what moral standards I hold and to what I do about them. It is in this sense that I deny that objective relativism is disastrous for morality. My dispute with the objectivists is not about whether moral standards are rooted in the nature of things. I believe that they are. My reservations have to do with the nature of our knowledge of those independently existing values and principles. Of what practical value is it to know or believe that moral values are rooted in reality? Some, if not most, of the fiercest disputes are not about whether morality is grounded in reality but about what reality requires of us. We all act on our beliefs. If all the objectivists were converted to my point of view, would it change in the slightest what they believe to be right and wrong? Would it change one bit how they actually live? I contend that it would not.

Two objectivists screaming at each about abortion from opposite extremes of the issue, each one certain that the other is absolutely wrong, is not a pretty sight. Of what value in a practical sense is their objectivism? It matters a lot whether they take a pro-choice or a pro-life position in politics and what actions they take in support of their convictions. It matters not at all that they are both objectivists about morality. Neither would it matter practically if one were an objectivist and the other a relativist. Claiming to have certain knowledge does not guarantee that one does. I agree that everyone ought to act upon his/her moral beliefs and fight for them in every appropriate way. But once I have decided that I am an objective relativist, I am not obligated to do anything further. I may choose to write articles and books about the subject and argue with others about the issue — and have fun doing it. But that has little to do with anything practical that affects the quality of life for the oppressed or the hungry or anyone else with real needs. It is in that sense that I contend that our moral beliefs and whether we act upon them matter greatly, but our beliefs about those beliefs do not. More specifically, disputes on metaethical questions matter only in theoretical thought as distinct from practical life in which thought wrestles with issues that demand choice and action and maybe the spilling of blood when fundamental issues of survival and justice hang in the balance.

Descriptions of reality and prescriptions about right and wrong do not float down from heaven while angels sing. They are created on earth by people. Rival claims are tested by human agents. Societies and individuals say what the world is like and what our obligations are. Truths are pronounced by human beings, reflecting their culture or their own peculiar personal slant on things. Errors are specified by somebody, some individual, some institution, or some group. Hence, all assertions about reality and morality are relative to the interpreting agent reflecting a particular cultural location in time and space. Neither human reason nor divine revelation provides an escape from this predicament. Believing that one or the other does settles nothing.

The decisive point is that the only access to reality we have is through "interprience," i.e., some interpretation of the experience of reality made by some interpreter.[3] For the moment I am putting aside the claim that divine revelation provides us with truth not given to interprience. Each interpretive outlook originates in and is reflective of some particular time and place. This does not necessarily mean that one cannot be translated into the language of another. But they do differ in method and content from other ways of believing produced by other groups, individuals, institutions, sacred books, prophets, philosophers, or found on tablets of stone alleged to be divinely authored. We cannot adjudicate rival and contrary claims to truth by comparing them with reality itself, since it is available to us only in some version produced by some human agency. We need some experience-interpretation scheme that is itself not just another version of truth but truth-itself. That is exactly what we do not and cannot have and know that we have it. No supreme court is available to make a final resolution, since any court consulted has nothing to offer but one more relative scheme. No escape from this epistemological predicament exists, except in the minds of the more confident who simply pronounce themselves to be in possession of the truth about things, i.e., a correct interpretation, not just one more relative effort. This is a victory over relativism by sheer declaration.

Hence, whether or not the distinction between conceptual scheme and content can be sustained,[4] a plurality of moral visions compete for our allegiance, each one dependent on some temporal-social location and some human agency. Much overlapping and large ranges of agreement can, of course, be found, even though the centers of competing circles of interpretation are at different points. Those who hold to one perspective may pronounce the others to be inferior or wrong, but such pronouncements are themselves part of some interpretive scheme and thus marked with the same kind of relativity as those judged to be in error. One of them may actually have it right, i.e., correctly represent or correspond with reality. Our predicament is that we cannot know for sure which one that is. Hence, we can only act on the one that is most convincing to us. When confronted with moral perspectives that are different from ours, we have two choices. (1) We can regard them as we would tastes in art or wines or colors as merely different from ours — and maybe even abhorrent to us — but not requiring any other response other than possibly to appreciate the variety that adds spice to life. (2) We can judge the differences to be of such importance that we must contend for our beliefs in the public arena against rival views, using whatever means are appropriate to prevail against them. This is the ultimate practical issue. To be paralyzed and unable to take a stand, act, or fight for causes we believe in is neither a necessary nor a responsible way to deal with relativism. In short, to say that all interpretive schemes are relative is not to vitiate them as guides to moral action that people can live by and act upon with energy and courage.

The standard objection to relativism is that it of necessity involves or leads to or is accompanied by assumptions and claims that have to be understood in a non-relative way. The simplest version of this refutation is that the assertion that all points of view are relative implies that relativity as a point of view is relative too and not a universal or objective truth. Put differently, relativity to be meaningful and worthy of consideration must be asserted in an objectivist sense, i.e., as a claim about things as they really are that logically excludes contrary views. If true, the claim itself establishes at least one objective fact and hence is self-refuting. If it is not true, it can be dismissed. A variant maintains that any statement said to be relative must unavoidably be supported by other statements or principles or background assumptions that transcend relativism and hence have a universal and objective status.[5]

The task of spelling out the case against relativism in detail and of responding to it adequately is beyond the scope of the present undertaking. The notion that relativism is logically self-refuting was made at least as far back as Plato against Protagoras (*Theaetetus*). Versions of the notion that relativism cannot establish the truth of its own position without refuting itself have been made ever since. It is of interest that despite this alleged mortal blow relativism lives even today. This may suggest that at least some relativists are getting at something that is not being refuted and that the critics are missing. My present conclusion is that granting even the most generous assessment of its validity, the case against relativism is not sufficient to undermine its essential claims. Whatever concessions must be made about the limitations and qualifications of some forms of relativism, the central point that systems of ethics and metaphysics can only be established or refuted by the truth-finding and truth-testing resources available to a given interpreter is not vitiated. If anyone thinks that the Thomistic proofs for the existence of God can be proven to be or not be in correspondence with reality, let that person come forth with the procedures that can objectively accomplish this feat. Any proposal made for this purpose will be rejected by objectivists who hold contrary positions and regarded as one more relative scheme by relativists. The essential question is whether relativism can be refuted when topics like this are at stake, not whether the affirmation of relativism is itself an absolute claim that is not self-sustaining. Nor is the crucial issue whether one must presuppose the rules of logic, freedom, causality, the passage of time, that some things are better than others, that some real things exist not presently being experienced, that life is meaningful, and the like. I do agree that principles of logic and perhaps some common-sense presuppositions about the nature of the world must be agreed to if any rational thought is to be carried on. Certainly no principles can be affirmed if the affirmation is self-refuting or denied if the denial by necessity presupposes them. Nevertheless, even if one acknowledged that some such set of allegedly universal, foundational beliefs cannot be rationally denied, that would not go very far toward a refutation of the form of relativism I defend.

The following reply could be made to the charge that if relativism is true, it is false. A statement about the nature of some other statements may have a different logical status from the other statements referred to. If so, the statement would not be self-contradictory, since it would not belong to the class of statements described by it. In other words, while statements about morality and religion are relative, the statement that these statements are relative may not be relative. Hence, even if the statement that some statements are relative is said to be absolute, this does not mean that the statements claimed to be relative are not relative. I will leave it to the logicians to determine whether some such reply to the charge that relativism is self-refuting can be sustained. However, the crucial point I want to make is that I do not have a theory that relativism is true. Specifically, I do not assert as a truth corresponding to reality that all claims about morality and religion are merely reflective of social location and therefore no one of them corresponds to reality. To do so would require me to be able to examine all versions of truth in the light of reality itself to see if they are all fundamentally determined by the time, place, and cultural orientation rather than by reality itself and thereby discover that no one of them correctly describes it. That is precisely what cannot be done. I am a relativist in that I maintain that what one sees depends on where one stands when looking. One has to describe what one sees with the categories at hand or that can be created at that time and place. All interpretations of reality can only employ the language at hand, available to, or obtainable by the interpreter. Moreover, they can be tested only by criteria that are themselves part of the interpretation. This would seem to be obvious, a mere truism. To deny this would require one to say that interpretations of morality and religion can use language and employ methods of justification not known or not available to the interpreter.

This does not exclude the possibility that some relative view may be absolutely right. While what one sees may be dependent on where one stands (the meaning of relativism), somebody may actually be standing at a place where he/she can get a clear, accurate, and complete view of the object in question (God, the moral order, e.g.). The problem is knowing for sure which, if any, of the many competing versions is based on that kind of perfect vision. I insist that no one can be certain that any interpretation corresponds to reality when we are talking about certain matters of epistemology, metaphysics, morality, and religion. Hence, total subjective confidence that a moral belief corresponds to reality is no guarantee that it does or even a reason to believe that it does, although the belief might be true. In other words, I am a skeptic. Is my skepticism justified? I am not certain that it is. In the final analysis relativism and skepticism are a simple confession that I am not sure that my views or those of anyone else tell it like it is in matters of metaphysics, epistemology, morality, and religion. I can only acknowledge what I believe, what I cannot deny, what I am fully persuaded of. If the subjective confidence that some have that their views correspond with reality turns out to be justified when we all get to epistemological heaven where all truth is revealed to all, it will have been a matter of luck. It would not necessarily mean that their certainty was objectively justified before the Last Day when all contenders finally learn once and always who was right and who was wrong and in what respects.

To put it differently, I am trying to avoid the necessity of affirming as objective truth corresponding to reality either that true moral beliefs are found or that all moral beliefs are merely made by their creators. I want to avoid and to transcend this dichotomy. I just say that I believe there is an objective moral and that true moral beliefs would mirror it. But I cannot be sure that this is the case or know with certainty that any of my specific moral views are representative of that objective order. Moral truth is found, but all actual beliefs about moral truth are created out of materials indigenous to some temporal-social-cultural location. All of this is a confession of the beliefs which guide me in theory and practice. I affirm them because they seem right to me. They account more adequately for more evidence than any alternative known to me, and they serve as a useful and so far satisfactory way of conducting myself as a morally seriously person who cares about justice and wants to make life better for myself and others.

When Correspondence Theory Holds And When It Doesn't

Relativism applies especially to systems of morality, religion, and metaphysics that point toward ultimate facts, values, purposes, and meanings ingredient in the fundamental nature of things. Within this context relative means dependent on and limited by the inventory of truth-finding and truth-testing resources available at a given time and place to a particular interpreter. Alfred North Whitehead in *Process and Reality* may have given a correct picture in its main outlines of the nature of the world and God as they really are. But how can we know whether he did or not? Different judgments will be made by logical positivists, Thomists, Hindus, orthodox Christians, and so on. Each of these perspectives illustrates relativity in the sense defined. When all is said and done, who is right? All the interpreters think they are. I say we can't be sure. Hence, the relativism I defend resolves finally into a form of skepticism that leads to a version of pragmatism for resolution of questions of meaning, morality, purpose, and metaphysical ultimacy.

In ordinary life, however, we can decide conclusively whether certain assertions correspond with reality for all practical purposes. If I say, "The broom is in the closet," it is possible, once the terms and particulars of the case have been defined and specified, to determine with certainty and finality in terms that everyone understands whether the broom meant is in the closet designated or not. Within the context in which this sentence is uttered, the broom is the reality that the speaker had in mind and the word broom corresponds to it in a sense that everyone recognizes in practice.

With regard to the simple matters of everyday life, then, the relations among reality, experience, and interpretation give us little practical difficulty, although philosophers will never settle the issue at the level of technical epistemological theory. Unfortunately,

not all disputes are as easily resolved. We could lay out a series of propositions ranging from non-controversial matters of fact in which the correspondence theory of truth is perfectly serviceable for practical purposes to the final facts about ultimate reality in which it becomes increasingly non-useful and finally pragmatically irrelevant. The following list will suffice:
1. The Atlanta Braves won the World Series in 1995.
2. The causes of the French Revolution were ...
3. Homosexual behavior is morally wrong.
4. God has a primordial nature (Whitehead).
5. God is one substance existing in three persons (Trinity).
6. Quarks and electrons exist in nature and are not simply part of the currently reigning scientific paradigm that is useful for certain purposes, including making predictions.

Proposition 1 is simply true in a sense that everyone understands, regardless of what theory of truth one holds. I maintain that it corresponds to reality in a practical sense even if my definition of "correspondence" could not be sustained theoretically to everyone's satisfaction. No definition, of course, would satisfy Richard Rorty. Proposition 2 is much less open to finality and certainty. While relevant facts are publicly available, the outcome depends on the assumptions held by a given interpreter, how the evidence is weighed, how many relevant facts are known, and much else. Not least is the troublesome question as to what causality means when speaking of historical events and to whether it is even a useful concept in this context. We could also debate the question as to whether there is such a thing as "The French Revolution" with a precise location in time and space as opposed to a series of events more or less identifiable that changed the lives of French people in substantial and long-lasting ways. The moral argument about 3 involves facts, principles, and values that are accessible to all interested parties and intelligible to all, although the outcome depends on some frame of reference relative to the interpreter. Followers of Alfred North Whitehead would maintain that reason and experience can provide evidence relevant to the determination of the truth of 4, but only those within the Whiteheadian camp will be persuaded — a tiny minority illustrating relativity at its finest. Christians have typically said that the doctrine of the Trinity is given in special divine revelation and is not a truth that can be established or refuted by reason, although it intends to describe objective reality. Theologians, of course, debate endlessly about what the orthodox formula means or just what the formula should be, or whether it even makes sense. Christians cannot resolve the issue among themselves in ways that elicit universal agreement. Among modern secularists the whole thing seems preposterous. Proposition 6 is only slightly less esoteric than 5 since only trained scientists know what is meant by quarks and electrons. Scientists have ways to decide whether theories about quarks and electrons can be sustained, but the dispute about their status in nature is as irresolvable as 5. Philosophers of science may never stop arguing about the best way to understand scientific theories.

The point is that relativity has different meanings depending on the context. It is negligible in 1, since anyone who understands the meaning of the terms in this English sentence can be persuaded of its absolute truth as a description that corresponds with reality in a sense that ordinary people and even philosophers when they are at home or off duty or try real hard fully understand. The sentence is simply true in a sense that we all grasp perfectly well for all practical purposes. In that sense it is probably true that most beliefs people hold are true, since they are similar in character to Proposition 1. Propositions 2, 3, and 4 depend on assumptions, methods of inquiry, weighing of evidence, and much else besides reflective of particular interpreting agents occupying different circles of interpretation. Disputes might arise over the "facts" as well as over the interpretation of the "facts." Where one comes out depends on where one stands and how one proceeds to reach conclusions. Universal agreement about what is objectively true may never come about regarding 2, probably not with respect to 3, and almost certainly not with 4. Few, if any, would claim that 5 can even be discussed apart from Christian traditions, documents, and experiences. Proposition 6 will doubtless remain in dispute between the realists and the pragmatists as long as Christians feud over the Trinity.

I have stirred around in the mire of epistemological debate enough to know that few claims are free from controversy. I make no pretense of having given a complete inventory or classification of statements and to the corresponding questions of justification associated with them. Language is far too complex and difficult a subject for it to be treated in a few paragraphs, even I were competent to do so. The few statements offered do, I hope, serve to make the point that beginning with a class of statements that can be verified conclusively to everybody's practical satisfaction, we can move to other categories of statements that cannot. Included in my small list are factual, historical, moral, metaphysical, and scientific claims, each of which poses its own perplexing issues with respect to the logic of meaning, truth, and verification. Not only do the issues of observational fact become more complex, but other peculiar problems arise, such as what "cause" means with respect to some events in history in relation to others. Even when observing a broom, no agreement exists about what is contributed to the observation by the observer (the mind or subject) and by what is observed (the thing or the object). If we raise the question as to what the "broom" really is in and of itself apart from its being humanly observed and named, a thousand theories bloom in metaphysical splendor with no consensus in sight. With respect to morality a distinction arises between "fact" and "value." The claim that homosexuality is wrong cannot be tested in the same way that the statement "broom in the closet" can. Some facts are relevant to the discussion, and debate about the matter is possible in that reasons can be given for or against the proposition. But neither human reason nor divine revelation can settle the issue since what reason demands us to say or what God has to say is always dependent on some reasoner or interpreter of divine opinion. Endless debate goes on with respect to the connections, identities, differences, and possibilities of convertibility between "fact" and "value" or between "is" and "ought." Metaphysical claims raise a still different set of issues regarding justification. In addition, there is the preliminary question as to whether the enterprise itself is impossible and irrelevant or necessary and inevitable. Nevertheless, I hope I have made the basic point that relativism takes on different meanings depending on the context. With regard to some simple statements of fact, it is negligible. In other types of statements the perspective of the interpreter related to the time, place, and social location of the interpreting agent becomes ever more determinative.

I have written on subjects in theology, ethics, and philosophy and developed an outlook at least in minimalist terms that is to me convincing.[6] My intention is to describe reality, to lay out propositions that correspond to or represent the objectively existing state of affairs. Yet such is the depth of my acknowledgment of relativism and skepticism that I do not find it useful to ask whether statements about God, the meaning of life, and the moral obligations of human beings even approximately represent things as they are. Nonrelativists who hold certain positions with great confidence have no alternative but to say that those who disagree with them are wrong. I am not prepared to say that those who disagree with me on moral, metaphysical, and religious matters are wrong. I just say I see it differently and will act on my own convictions in appropriate ways, and that includes opposing those who differ with means proportionate to the seriousness of the issue. I also assume that every other religious, moral, and metaphysical claim is no less relative in principle than mine. Relativism, however, does not preclude passion, commitment, and action in line with one's own relative viewpoint. It ideally produces humility accompanied by acts of love in the quest for justice and an openness to deeper insight.

Moreover, in my view, all claims about morality and religion can be tested by myself and others but without certain or absolutely conclusive results. The first criterion is theoretical. I can employ the rational test of coherence (internal consistency with all other propositions I affirm) and the empirical test of evidence (adequacy in accounting for the full range of experience). Yet I know that however successful I may be in applying these tests of truth, the outcome is such that only one who stands where I stand will see what I see. All I can say is that this is the best I have been able to come up with so far. Methods of justifying claims are internal to the point of view being tested and part of it, so that no method provides a way of escaping the relativity that marks all belief systems.

The second and most important test is practical. Is the outlook useful in interpreting the whole range of my experience in an adequate (rationally plausible) way and in providing guidance in coping with life? When I live by what I find convincing as a rational being, are the results satisfactory and satisfying judged by the best standards available to me up to now as I continue to learn and revise both my theory and my practices? One hopes that learning, maturity, and experience will lead to increasingly adequate and fulfilling ways of believing and living, loving and hoping, thinking and acting. In the end I am a pragmatist who in the presence of the ultimate questions abandons the hope of knowing with certainty what the ultimate answers are. Nevertheless, I find in my own outlook a way of thinking and living more useful and productive than any alternatives available to me at this time. Are my religious and moral convictions literally true? Do they correspond with reality? These questions are interesting but futile. It would be the greatest miracle of all time if out of all the religions and philosophies ever produced on this earth, it turned out that my own was the closest of any to getting it right, telling it like it is, picturing objective reality so that the picture and pictured are remarkably alike! Could not the same be said in principle for the chances of Plato, Confucius, Aquinas, Ayer, Rorty, or anyone else you want to name, even allowing for their greater mental acumen? Yet I must live some way, believe something, hope for what seems most likely, and die trusting it was not all in vain. I proceed, then, as a relativist, a pragmatist, and a skeptic who employs correspondence theory as far as it will take me, but beyond the ordinary facts of everyday life, that is not very far, especially when one enters the realms of morality and religion.

The Content Of Belief And The Status Of Belief

With this in mind, let me return to the original thesis. I have distinguished between the content of moral judgments (beliefs) and the status of moral judgments (beliefs about those beliefs).[7] The former matters in that it is the stuff and arena of debate between competing outlooks. The latter does not. Consider three sets of propositions:

I. Objectivism

A. Gratuitous cruelty is wrong.
B. We are obligated to prevent it wherever possible.
C. The first two propositions are universally valid, objective truths whether anyone believes them to be true or not. They are found not made, discovered not created.
D. I believe A and B and will live by them.

II. Objective Relativism

A. Gratuitous cruelty is wrong.
B. We are obligated to prevent it wherever possible.
C. The first two propositions follow from my philosophy of life, but I have no way of knowing whether they mirror objective reality or not. However, I believe that they do.
D. I believe A and B and will live by them.

III. Subjective Relativism

A. Gratuitous cruelty is wrong.
B. We are obligated to prevent it wherever possible.
C. The first two propositions are valid only for those cultures or individuals who affirm them. They are made not found, created by people, not discovered in reality.
D. I accept A and B and will live by them.

For objectivists (Position I) A and B state objective truths, so that anyone who denies them is just plain wrong, i.e., out of tune with reality. Objective relativists (Position II) like me would say that we believe that A and B are objective truths, but we do not know for sure whether those who deny them are wrong or not, but we will act as if they are. Subjective relativists (Position III) maintain that A and B are opinions or customs or feelings only, so that the question of objective right and wrong is not an issue. For them right and wrong do not exist somewhere in reality independently of subjective beliefs, values, feelings, and preferences. Moreover, the subjective relativist interprets obligation differently from the other two. For the objectivists and the objective relativist obligation refers to a felt necessity to be obedient to an order of rightness grounded in the nature of things. For the subjective relativist it is a self-generated or internalized felt oughtness to live in conformity with one's own culture, convictions, feelings, or preferences.

About this scheme I draw two conclusions:
1. C is not the same kind of claim as A and B. Put most simply, A and B are beliefs. C is a belief about beliefs.
2. A and B matter (have practical consequences). C as such does not (has no necessary practical consequences).

The crucial question is whether some types of C belief about A and B are essential to sustain D commitments. My answer is no. How moral standards and commitments are generated and sustained is a different question and is logically independent of beliefs about beliefs. Someone who holds Position III might choose to regard the good of others as equal to his or her own and live accordingly. An objectivist who agrees that moral standards have a grounding in reality might choose to live a self-centered life. Augustinian Christian orthodoxy, an objectivist position if there ever were one, says that in fact that is what we in fact all do. We could, I suppose, argue about whether III has a stronger gravitational pull in that direction or not, but it is not a necessary implication of III any more than a belief in the objectivity of moral standards guarantees a virtuous life. I do not believe that holding Position III is necessarily deleterious to just and benevolent living, but I would be willing to submit the question for empirical testing and would admit to being wrong if the evidence refuted me. I would expect, however, that if objectivists were found to live by different moral standards, it would be for reasons other than C type beliefs about A type moral issues. Furthermore, until refuted by clear empirical evidence, I will insist that objectivism is no guarantee either of superior moral ideals or of lives more in conformity with professed standards than what is to be found in the lives of relativists. I am not forgetting that I am a relativist, so I readily acknowledge that any judgment about superior morality is made from a particular point of view.

To make the point another way, I can imagine two slaveholders, one of whom is an objectivist and the other a subjective relativist. The objectivist might appeal to reason (Aristotle) and revelation (the Bible) to show that slavery was right by objective standards.

The subjective relativist might eschew that kind of talk and say simply that slavery is the way we do things in this society, and he/she personally approves and has very strong positive feelings about it and will defend it by all necessary means. Likewise, I can image two abolitionists, one of whom is an objectivist and the other a subjective relativist. The objectivist might appeal to natural law and to the highest principles of Scripture to oppose slavery, maintaining that nature and God pronounce it wrong. The subjective relativist might simply find it personally offensive and repugnant, neither worrying nor caring what the objective order of reality requires, insisting that life in a society free of slavery is merely preferable for purely discretionary reasons.

It is not belief about the status of ethical beliefs that determines either the content of moral standards or the commitment to live by them. Moral choice is guided by character, and character is a product of nature (genes), nurture (family and culture), life experiences reflected upon, previous choices, and the like. Someone reared in a warm, loving family with clear moral values that are taken to be reflective of the nature of things is not likely to abandon them after taking a college course and converting to subjective relativism. That might happen, but I suspect it would not unless other and more decisive influences and events were at work as well. In any case, I insist that the final test is empirical. Let us examine the moral stances and actions of people and see what, if any, consequences follow as such from having one set of beliefs about beliefs rather than another or from changing from one position to another. I would expect to find that differences in moral belief and practice among people are rooted in other factors than whether they are objectivists or relativists.

Let us suppose that (1) my version of objective relativism is true, i.e., corresponds with reality. Further, let us suppose, however, that this point of view is not capable of generating passion and courage when the ultimate test comes, that it cannot produce a willingness to die for causes worthy of dying for. This means that the moral enterprise to be sustainable must be based on a lie. Let us suppose instead that (2) the objectivists are right and that relativism cannot sustain the moral enterprise. Then the objectivist has the burden not only of discovering the truth about particular moral issues (abortion, war, and the like) but also of persuading people to be objectivists, since the moral enterprise cannot be sustained otherwise. I do not believe either 1 or 2 describes the unhappy predicament we live in or that this is what is at stake in the argument between the objectivists and the relativists. Suppose finally that (3) objectivism is true but that both forms of relativism can support the moral enterprise in most people in the same ways and to the extent that objectivism can. Then my question is: What is all the fuss about? What is at stake in the argument? If the acceptance of objectivism or relativism makes no practical difference in what we actually believe to be right and good or in the way we sincerely and passionately commit ourselves to those beliefs, then in a pragmatic sense, it does not matter whether you are an objectivist or not. That suggests to me that we all should turn our attention to discovering what is right and good and in nurturing people so that they live by their convictions and not worry about what theory of truth they hold.

Some Theses About Relativism And Ethics

The following propositions follow from what has been said so far:

1. Universal agreement does not guarantee objective rightness. If everyone agreed that it was all right to torture babies just for the fun of it, that would not make it right.
2. The mere fact of disagreement, no matter how great, does not disprove the theory of objective rightness. Hence, the fact that a plurality of moral views can be found among various cultures and among individuals within the same culture does not in itself establish the truth of subjective relativism.
3. Objective relativism does not forbid me from holding that views different from mine are wrong. I merely say they are wrong from my perspective or that I believe they are wrong. If relativism means that one idea, value, or practice is about as good as any other, then I am most certainly not a relativist. It would be hard to find a relativist thus

defined, other than Richard Rorty's "cooperative freshman." My intention is to make claims about morality and religion that are true (correspond with reality), and some of them might be. But my views could also be wrong. I believe that some courses of action are objectively superior to others. But which ones? And how do we know? These are the troublesome questions. To answer mine is the right one, and it is right because I perceive the truth correctly will not suffice, since that is, after all, what the argument is about.

4. Objective relativism denies that two contrary views can be equally valid, but validity is always a judgment made from some relative perspective. For subjective relativists validity, if used at all, only means that some group or individual prefers or is committed to or lives by a particular set of standards. Even here two conflicting norms would not necessarily be regarded as equally valid for them by the same group or individual.

5. In cases of genuine ambiguity, of course, two courses of action might be equally valid. It might be that both will achieve equivalent mixtures of good and evil (teleological) or are equally reflective of the order of moral obligation (deontological), there being no preferable third course of action available. For example, in a particular instance getting a divorce or staying married may result in equal amounts of harm and good, though perhaps distributed in different ways. Here validity is judged by the same moral principles representing one particular outlook. In a wider context, a pluralism of values must be acknowledged that does not allow a simple harmony among them or permit the realization of them all simultaneously in absolute fashion. They can be in conflict. Consider liberty and equality, freedom and order, justice and mercy, and unity and diversity, for example. The values in each of these pairs objectively considered constrain and relativize each other. Sometimes, at least, to get more of one, we have to have less of the other.[8]

6. Absolute subjective confidence in the validity of one's moral beliefs does not guarantee that they correspond with reality. Certitude about them is a basis for acting upon beliefs but is not proof that they are in harmony with the nature of things. If someone believed beyond the shadow of a doubt that torturing babies for the fun of it was okay with the universe or God or Reality or whatever, that would not make it so.
7. Objective relativism does not preclude rational debate with objectivists about ethics. Discussion can include what makes something right or wrong as well as particular matters of morals such as abortion, assisted suicide, and affirmative action. Contending parties can lay out their assumptions and claims along with supporting evidence. Suspected errors of fact, logic, and relevance can be indicated, debated, and refuted. Circles of interpretation will exhibit various degrees of overlapping along with divergence. The disputants can reach a large measure of understanding about the basis for agreement and disagreement. Sometimes persuasive argument will lead to a revision of outlook. Perhaps some positions will approach incommensurability with others, but the reasons for this dissonance can be explored. What reason cannot do is mark out a methodological path that if followed by all competent, rational pursuers of truth will lead eventually to universal conclusions that can be doubted only by defying reason itself.
8. Relativism does not logically imply that "might makes right." In the absence of objectively valid standards by which moral practices can be appraised, critics aver that relativism means in effect that the distinction between is and ought vanishes so that what prevails, prevails. Whatever customs or preferences establish themselves and root out all others by whatever means determines what is, and that is all that can be said about the matter. In reply it can be noted that prevailing and rightness are not the same thing. Moreover, objectivism does not logically exclude the view that "might is right" and relativism does not necessarily imply it. Some objectivists

have argued that survival of the strongest is a law of nature, so that no moral objection can be made to their domination. Objectivist relativists may believe that love, not power, is the supreme moral principle. Even subjective relativists could insist on the difference between what is and what they prefer. Hence, no necessary connection exists in theory or practice between might and right for either objectivists or relativists. If, however, subjective relativism is more prone in any sense toward the notion that "might makes right," then so be it. I do not need to defend against it. I am an objective relativist who thinks might is might and right is right, and the one cannot be reduced to the other.

Conclusion

My present moral beliefs rest on the assumption that we live in the presence of a Divine Creativity that is the source of life and that aims at the fullest possible actualization of enjoyment for all living creatures. This is the foundation of morality. Our calling is to respond to God in ways that promote the fulfillment of all that lives, especially human beings. As I come better to appreciate who I am and the meaning and purpose of my existence in the larger scheme of things, I may change my mind about that and about what obligations and duties are incumbent upon me. That would matter, would have practical consequences. I could also change my mind about the status of my beliefs and become an objectivist, but I doubt if that would matter much one way or the other beyond the fact of the intellectual conversion itself. Much philosophical discussion is concerned with getting the status of theory correct and does not ask often enough what the practical implications are. I, on the other hand, want to keep asking one question: So what? What difference does it make in experience? With William James I contend that if it does not make a difference in experience, then the differences may be interesting but not very important.

In the following chapter, I will compare my views with those of Richard Rorty, to whom I am quite close, and point out where I think his form of relativism is inadequate.

Endnotes

1. For a good survey of philosophical options in epistemology from Plato to Putnam, see Paul K. Moser and Arnold Vander Nat, eds., *Human Knowledge: Classical and Contemporary Approaches* (New York: Oxford University Press, 1987). So far as I can tell, the main lesson to be learned from this splendid volume is that for every cogent position offered, at least two equally cogent refutations are generated, giving rise to still further attempts to work out the difficulties thought to vitiate previous efforts.

2. The difference between a belief and a belief about belief is not always clear. Consider these two statements. (1) What cannot be known by scientific methods not only cannot be known but is not real. (2) The preceding statement is true in the sense that it corresponds to reality. I call (1) a belief and (2) a belief about belief. Statement 1 asserts something believed to be true (content of belief). Statement 2 affirms something about the nature of truth (status of belief).

3. It actually is more complicated than this. My view is that at its base reality consists of nothing but experiencers and their experiences. I am a panpsychist in the vicinity of the views of Alfred North Whitehead. For any experiencer reality is what it is experienced as. Hence, I am also close to the pragmatism and empiricism of William James. Our interpretations of our experience may be wrong, i.e., inconsistent with subsequent or other experiences. Interpretations, then, are subject to revision. A duck may experience a sound, interpret it to be coming from another duck, and move in that direction only to experience disastrous results when it turns out that the sound was made by a hunter. An objective order is real, but it is not easy to say what it is that is real other than to say it is what some experiencer experiences it as and interprets it to be. Apart from its being experienced, perhaps the best we can say is that to be objectively real is to have the power or capacity to affect something or to be affected. See my *Theological Biology: The Case for a New Modernism* (Lewiston, NY: Edwin Mellen Press, 1991), 65-120, and *Toward a New Modernism* (Lanham, MD: University Press of America, 1997), 116-24.

4. Donald Davidson maintains that it cannot. See Donald Davidson, "On the Very Idea of a Conceptual Scheme," in *Inquiries into Truth and Representation* (Oxford: at the Clarendon Press, 1984), 183-98. Scheme and content may not be separable from or independent of each other, but the content of an outlook may involve assumptions, presuppositions, and may have implications necessary to its meaning, and this structural whole containing the assumptions, presuppositions, and implications existing in indissoluble unity with the content may be thought of as the conceptual scheme in distinction from the particulars of its content.

5. See Thomas Nagel, *The Last Word* (New York: Oxford University Press, 1997), and David Griffin in *Varieties of Postmodern Theology* (Albany: State University of New York Press, 1989). Obviously an extreme form of subjective relativism that affirms that conflicting claims can be true, i.e., true for those who believe it, is easily refuted.

6. For my ethical and metaethical theory, *Process Ethics: A Constructive System* (Lewiston, NY: Edwin Mellen Press, 1984) is especially important.

7. For a long, convoluted, and unconvincing argument denying the validity of this distinction, see Ronald Dworkin, "Objectivity and Truth," *Philosophy and Public Affairs*, vol. 25, no. 2 (Spring 1996), 87-139. Dworkin insists that to say that a statement corresponds with reality is just a way restating, repeating, or emphasizing the statement itself, not a logically different kind of statement. Take the following sentences: (1) Abortion is wrong. (2) It is true that abortion is wrong, it really is. (3) The statement that abortion is wrong corresponds with reality. According to Dworkin all these sentences mean the same thing. This is the case only if one assumes it to be so. Compare 3 with another statement. (4) The statement that abortion is wrong means that abortion is disapproved in society X, nothing more. Here it is evident that 1, 3, and 4 are not all identical. Correspondence to reality is one option among others for defining what moral statements mean. Hence, I persist in suggesting that a distinction can be made between beliefs and beliefs about beliefs.

8. Isaiah Berlin spoke of three propositions that have been dominant in the mainstream of Western tradition: (1) All genuine questions have one answer that is true for everybody, everywhere, all the time. (2) A path leading to the discovery of these truths is in principle available to everyone. (3) All truths are compatible and form one harmonious whole. See Michael Ignatieff, *Isaiah Berlin: A Life* (New York: Metropolitan Books, 1998). In part, it depends on what 1 means. If it means there is no one perfect, conflict-free moral ideal absolutely valid for all societies, I agree. There may be equally excellent but different ways of organizing the plurality of values in line with 3. However, there may be some universal truths about reality that allow only one right answer, so I am not sure that 1 is altogether objectively wrong. The problem is knowing what the one true answer for all questions is. Hence, I agree wholeheartedly in rejecting 2 in accordance with my understanding of relativism. With respect to 3 as far as ethics is concerned, I agree with Berlin in affirming a stubborn pluralism that insists that not all moral values can be realized simultaneously in individuals or societies without qualification, conflict, or limitation.

Chapter 3

Telling It Like It Is — Can We? Reasoning With Rorty

Since my version of relativism and pragmatism has many points of contact with the writings of Richard Rorty, it may be useful to explore this relationship in more detail. Rorty is well-known for declaring that the epistemological project is a failure.[1] In *Philosophy and the Mirror of Nature*, he declares as bankrupt the long tradition that seeks to construct sentences that correctly represent the way things are. The mind does not mirror the structure and patterns of the world, does not give us the truth about reality but only interpretations. These linguistic formulations can be tested only by their usefulness, not by their representation of the way things are. Philosophers can only use the language and concepts available to them in their time and place. Truth, reality, nature, essence, value, and the like are given their meaning by the current consensus of the users of those terms. Science has no privileged status as the path to knowledge about things as they are. It is one of many communities with a particular set of linguistic practices used to describe the world. What science defines as reality means only that version of the world that scientists currently agree to, which may or may not change over time. That we believe in democracy and human rights has no deeper source than contingent facts of history having to do with when and where we were born. Anything that we can convince others to believe will flourish to that extent.

Philosophical debate is not constrained or determined by reality or by the mind but only by what we or others consent to. No limits to conversation exist except what others will allow us to say.

Over time new ways of speaking are introduced, and the language games go on endlessly. Philosophers cannot prove they are telling the truth about reality, since reality is available only in the interpretations they or others give of it. Claims can be refuted only by using other words that are themselves caught up in an inescapable predicament of circularity. Justification depends on being able to test interpretations by comparing them to reality, while reality is available only in interpretations that are to be tested. The only way to resolve disputes would be to compare truth claims with reality as it is in itself to see how accurate they are, but bare, naked, non-interpreted reality as it really is prior to and apart from its linguistic description is not available to us. He does not say reality is not there or that there is no truth about it. He does not have a theory about truth or reality to replace the theories he is rejecting. Seeking objectivity can only mean getting as much intersubjective agreement as possible. The appearance-reality distinction is replaced with a contrast between the less useful and more useful.

Rorty denies that he is a relativist instead of an objectivist.[2] He means he does not have a theory that claims relativism is true. He just wants to change the subject. His point is to abandon all theories about truth and reality and to turn to edifying conversations that might be useful in helping us cope better with life. Truth is not a deep subject about which much of interest can be said.[3] All the debates in the past from Plato on about Truth, Goodness, Reality, and Moral Law by Philosophy have not paid off, and are not worth continuing. He capitalizes them to indicate the search for the ultimate nature of the world, the universal objective features — the Essence of things — built into reality itself that the mind is supposed to mirror. All such efforts by Philosophy are but the legacy of Plato and his Myth of the Cave, in which some fortunate souls escape from the moving shadows on the darkened wall to find Pure Knowledge of the Eternal Forms illumined by the Sun itself. Let us forget about theory and concentrate on practice.

Moral practice for Rorty means such things as combating cruelty and promoting a progressive agenda in politics that includes narrowing the wage gap, broadening civil rights, protecting the weak against the predatory practices of the strong, and generally reducing social injustice.[4] He thinks liberals, especially academic Leftists, should pay more attention to class than to culture, more to old-fashioned selfishness and greed that produces great economic inequalities and less to the personal slights, insults, stigmas, and exclusions that arise out of prejudice against certain groups. He wants to promote solidarity in which the "we" with which communities identify themselves comes to include more and more of humanity. The important question is not *what we are* but *who we are*. Let us not waste time worrying about the human essence or human nature and what is normative, right, and good for the kind of beings we are. The important question is who we include in the community of those we care about and are willing to sacrifice for.

Having trashed the epistemological project in Chapter 2 and declared it to be a total failure, I am not about to make an effort here to get it right at long last. Since eminent philosophers cannot even agree about how we know the ordinary things of everyday experience, much less whether God-talk is credible, it would be foolish for me to think I can walk through this mine field without being blown to pieces by anyone with the slightest familiarity of the issues. Have any two great minds ever agreed on every epistemological point since Plato's line and cave? I proceed only because I need for myself some way of organizing my own thoughts in a way that integrates as harmoniously as I can what I cannot at this moment doubt about such matters. It serves a useful purpose for me to try to put things together coherently in minimal fashion in my own mental universe. I don't expect it will work completely for anyone else, but here is the way it seems to me at the moment.

I find myself very close to Rorty's point of view. Sometimes I think I agree entirely. But some nagging thoughts remain. I find in myself an ineradicable need to find some place for reality reference in terms that intend to be true as well as useful — a distinction that he denies, even though I make it within a form of thoroughgoing relativism and skepticism. In some ways there is no point in debating with Rorty. He always has an answer within his frame of reference.[5] Any time anyone tries to get some objectivity back into the picture, he finds that the proposed solution does not work, is useless. It takes you back toward an indefensible foundationalism[6] and a futile Platonism and the effort to get to the last segments of the famous line of Plato that culminates in intellectual knowledge (*noēsis*) of the Forms. Probably the best thing to do is to take his advice and just change the subject.

However, many of us think there is a problem with respect to a public world that Rorty has not resolved, something beyond conversation and texts that the language employed is about.[7] I cannot do without objectivity in making sense of the total picture within my own frame of reference. For Rorty debates are about, are contained within, and never get beyond the encounter of one way of speaking with another. Changes in linguistic practices occur by some form of cultural mutation or internal evolution and spread as other speakers adopt the new words because they just seem better than the old. If speakers adopt new ways because they think they are more adequate to reality or the objective moral order, they are just fooling themselves. It is an illusion to think of a non-linguistic reality that can be spoken of without someone speaking of it. The object dissolves into the words that describe it. All we have is the identity of language and world, of the description and the described. The attempt to distinguish between reality and interpretation so that the latter can be assessed in terms of its adequacy to the former has not worked and should be abandoned. Analysis shows that it is language all the way down, and no matter how deep we go we cannot get to something that is not text but that to which the text is trying to correspond in some fashion. We cannot break out of language to compare it with something else. He does not deny that there is a world or an environment with which we are coping, yet the world can never be a theory-independent referent employed to assess theory since the uninterpreted world exists for us only as interpreted by one set of words or another.

Yet in the interplay of linguistic practices with each other, new vocabularies do emerge that are adopted according to Rorty not because they are more adequate to reality but are simply better tools for coping with the world. Language can be used to criticize language and to enlarge itself in the same way that exercise strengthens the body, but the comparisons are always between one set of linguistic practices and another but never between any vocabulary and the world. Language is the human way of coping as beavers use teeth to cut logs. It needs no justification beyond the fact that it works to help us cope, i.e., do the human equivalent of cutting logs.

He would certainly agree that sulphuric acid is not good to drink whereas orange juice is. I want to say this is true because the human body is what it is and that my thinking otherwise is objectively wrong (assuming one prefers life and health to a horrifying death). Even if he refers to consequences in experience as showing that some things work better than others, don't we need to ask why they work, in this case nourish the body instead of killing it? Is there not something about the objective nature of orange juice that in truth suits it better to the objective nature of the body rather better than sulphuric acid? My reading of him is that he would have two responses. (1) He thinks that to clarify and complete such claims about objectivity, nature, and so on, we need to say much more. No effort to provide the more is ever sufficient, never quite fills the bill. Besides that it gets us into all the interminable disputes over centuries of time about what reality really is and what adequate representation of it means that lead us inevitably toward an untenable distinction between reality and the language we use to describe it. (2) Such theories are no good anyway, not useful in helping us do anything practical. For Rorty the familiar world of people and things remains in all its variety, beauty and ugliness, and with all its disputes over moral values and social practices. However, it is enough, he thinks, to make the following kinds of statements, to take a few examples: The dog is chasing a rabbit. It was a good thing for Susan to leave her husband under the circumstances. A sharp metal axe is better than a blunt stone tool for cutting down trees. That picture is beautiful. We did the right (or wrong) thing in bombing Yugoslavia. Abortion can (or cannot) be justified in some circumstances. We can say many specific things about what is real, right, good, true, and beautiful without having to develop theories about the Real, the Moral Law, the Good, the True, and the Beautiful, and so on in the long shadow of Plato. He just prefers another way of putting it that is simpler and sufficient without going into all those unresolvable, worthless disputes.

The question then becomes in Rorty's view and mine whether given 1 and 2, it is worth continuing the objectivity enterprise. Rorty sets this issue within a larger context of what kind of culture we want. Do we want a post-philosophical one in which no special groups or disciplines have privileged status because they know how to discover the innermost Secret about the world? Or do we want a culture that continues the futile search for translinguistic objectivity? In the new civilization philosophy would look much like literature or culture criticism. Not even Science would be regarded as the source of the deepest Truth about the world. In a conversational culture each party to debates seeks to persuade others and thus to enlarge the community of those who consent to a particular vocabulary for describing the world or commending certain moral or social policies.

Rorty is quite clear about the implications of such a civilization. It would mean that when the torturers do their vicious work or the secret police come into the middle of the night to take the innocent, you cannot say to them that though they may have power forever, they are violating something deep in the universe and their own human nature. You cannot appeal to anything objective or universal in the moral order of reality to combat cruelty, injustice, or totalitarianism. The only points of reference for Rorty are speakers and the language they use to cope.

How can we respond to this challenge? I cannot escape the deep intuition that he is leaving out something that is essential. Many of us believe there are ways of avoiding the total dichotomy of Platonism and his version of pragmatism but not one that would persuade Rorty or gain universal consent. Davidson may be right that the distinction between conceptual scheme and content will not hold and that all claims made in one language may be fully translatable into every other language.[8] Whether this is true or not, the claims about the world people make do differ in assumptions, methods, and conclusions, and they are relative to time, place, and individual patterns of thought.[9] Let us grant that his view of what is better, just, and good and therefore worth promoting reflects his own way of looking at the world that is as historically and culturally accidental as he wants to make it. I will grant that no universal or objective claims can be made for this except within some particular frame of reference. However, if he can get passionate about his agenda though it is totally arbitrary and without any belief that his values have some grounding in something outside his own subjectivity, that is truly ironical! He might reply that my own relativism leads to an equally ironic set of passionate commitments. I agree with a pragmatism that refers to a continuing chain of learning in which we profit by previous experience in an ongoing history. I do not see why we cannot go on to claim that if certain consequences follow that constitute working satisfactorily, it may be because things are the way they are, although we can only describe the way things are within the linguistic framework we presently find convincing. Rorty, of course, would agree that we can, but in doing so, we are not adding anything worthwhile and nothing beyond a rhetorical pat on the back. Nevertheless, I cannot rid myself of the conviction that drinking orange juice has good consequences in experience because it has objective merit, i.e., is good, fitting, pleasurable, or satisfying, and suitable for the needs of the body in ways that are connected with the way the world is. This may be a purely empty and useless reference to the objective without practical importance in a general sense, but I need it for my own intellectual satisfaction within my own frame of reference. Such relativistic reference to the objective is pragmatically helpful to me.

It is easier, of course, to discern what is objectively appropriate when we are talking about food than when asking about the permissibility of abortion, affirmative action, justice in economic matters, intervention in Kosovo, and the like, but the question is still relevant. The good life has its objective requirements as well, bodily health being one component. We can claim that we are proposing what is objectively right and good given what human beings are and what fulfills them given their nature as we discern that in our own belief system. We cannot claim that we have correctly discovered the objective moral order but only that this is the best we know up to now but subject to future revision. Granted that we cannot confront reality as it in itself, but experience does provide clues to reality that we can interpret. We can never escape the circularity of reality, experience, and interpretation, but we can continue to revise our interpretation to gain greater adequacy to empirical evidence and greater coherence with our total system of ideas in enlarging bodies of interpretation. We can never escape the particularities of our linguistic practices in this quest. We can never have certainty that our interpretations of experience represent the world as it is independently of our theories about it. But we can achieve tentative bodies of interpretation that work for us in helping us cope with life and in learning how to live it better with broader and deeper ranges of satisfaction.

I think any account of experience is inadequate unless within experience it has some place for the objective — the what-is-not-us but is encountered by us and, admittedly, known to us only as we experience and interpret it. Rorty does agree that there is really a world that is not us, but it seems to me he does not deal adequately with the implications of that admission. Hence, he is close to being, in my terms, a subjective relativist. He can only claim that he believes what he believes and that he believes it because of purely arbitrary, accidental, historically contingent, or individually eccentric reasons. His preferences are thoroughly subjective and totally dependent on the particular circumstances that constitute his life history. He would appear to think that reason is utterly incompetent to think its way out of these constraints. If he believes that we cannot pronounce cruelty and outrageous atrocities against other people to be objectively wrong even if from only our standpoint, I find this a weak foundation on which to build a moral edifice worthy of living by. If he holds that such beliefs are merely our private fictions, then I demur. If reason has any ability to think itself beyond our present ideas, attitudes, feelings, and commitments, then surely the reasons we give for changing our minds for something better must refer to something really out there that makes the new alternative work more satisfactorily, granted that we can only interpret the out there (the world) by what is in here (the mind and its linguistic equipment). Does the total process go on within our heads and guts with never any correction or constraint from the world side of things? If theory is underdetermined by evidence, that we can grant, but is it totally underdetermined? If he is saying that when we confront the objective world, the only resources we have for making sense out of it all are those provided by our current linguistic habits, I agree. Let us grant that the red light is a "red light" only within my set of linguistic practices. Nevertheless, when I perceive it to turn from red to green, the new perception is caused by something that goes on in that whatever-it-really-is-in-the-nature-of-things apart from my knowledge of it that I call a "red light." Is there nothing analogous to this in the moral realm? I think there is some objectivity in our subjectivity. Rorty apparently thinks there is, but in the final analysis it seems to get dissolved into and identified with the language we use to describe it. This is where I want to say something more. He believes that the only reference is to experience as the testing ground of factual, scientific, and moral claims, so that we never need to go beyond experience itself to make any claims about what it is that is being experienced. But even so does not that require some understanding of the nature and structure of experience, its constituents, necessary conditions, and so on? Or can subject and object be overcome in pure experience so that experience itself is all that counts? That is a subject for continuing debate, I grant.

The challenge is to go beyond objectivism and subjective relativism. We can recognize cultural and individual relativity and the historicity of knowledge without giving up the quest for universal truth. Reality is not some unknown, unknowable something behind all knowing. It is known and knowable but only as experienced and interpreted. Reality is what it is known as (William James). This does not mean that reality is reduced to what is known or that it is real only as known. It is what it is, but it is known to us only in the knowing process. And it is for us what it is known as. We cannot conceptually compare our interpretive schemes directly to reality to see if they correspond to reality since the only thing we have to compare is one interpretive scheme with another one.

We can, however, debate as to whether one theory is a more adequate interpretation of the experienced reality than alternatives. Rorty is not far from what I have just claimed, but in the end the objective dimension seems to get swallowed up in the language and disappears. I want to say it is still there and accessible to some extent in and through the experience of it and the language we use to describe it. I agree what we can never say with certainty when we have gotten it completely right, especially when matters of morality and metaphysics are concerned. Yet this accessibility to the objective does provide a means of revisiting and correcting our interpretations. Rorty seems to me not to allow this to the extent and in the way that I do, if at all.

It is difficult to argue with Rorty because he disavows all the terms that come to mind as describing him from my point of view. He is in his own terms not a subjectivist, not a relativist. He just wants to change the subject, to speak of these matters in a different way. Theory change is not arbitrary or non-arbitrary. When it happens, it is just that people move from one set of linguistic practices to another. "Reality" is the way we currently describe things. "True" is what is good in the way of belief, useful in some context. "Good" is a description of what serves a purpose in some instance. "Right" is a name for what we approve judged by our present set of linguistic practices. He goes around and around in circular fashion without ever referring to anything beyond some way of speaking about it by some community or person. When one vocabulary is succeeded by another, notions of reliable objective criteria guiding theory choice simply do not come into play. The change cannot be said to be logical or illogical or made for objective, subjective, or arbitrary reasons. It is neither a matter of will nor of argument. The habit of using certain words is replaced by the practice of using other words. We don't justify liberal democracy. That is just the way we talk about politics. Linguistic habits mutate. They survive in the larger culture if they become the focus of a new consensus. This is a kind of evolutionary behaviorism in which we pay attention to the language evolution that actually occurs without being able or needing to judge whether the changes are good or bad as measured by some universal, objective standard. We can only say that some ways of viewing the world are more useful for achieving our purposes than others.

Rorty is denying the claim of the realist that it is useful to think that deep down beneath all language is something to which language is trying to be adequate. Nor is there any purpose for which we construct vocabularies or cultures to fulfill. All that can be said is that while playing one vocabulary off against another, we come up with new and better ways of speaking and acting. Better is not determined by measuring the new linguistic practices by some objective standard but in the sense that they just seem better, are more interesting to us, or work better for us. He affirms that there is indeed a world that is not linguistic. It can incite verbal behavior in us. But the experience is not such that we can refer to the world to test the adequacy of the language we currently use. Language is a tool human beings use to cope with life, but we can never separate the tool from its users to inquire about its adequacy to reality. All criteria we might use to test language as to its adequacy to reality are temporary stopping places constructed by some community to facilitate its inquiries and to achieve some specific utilitarian ends. They are needed to stop the infinite regress of inquiry, i.e., to get something done. No way has yet been found to think about the world or our purposes except by using our language. So we seem trapped in the language that is our tool for coping, but we do change vocabularies yet do so without any criteria that transcend the words we use. The tests are tests we impose, not tests that the world imposes. We can never transcend this predicament. In the end he seems to be saying that we can change our ways of speaking and writing only by adopting what is more interesting to us, that seems more useful as a coping device, that it is better in the last analysis because it seems better to us.

It is easy to forget and difficult to understand just what he is and is not saying. To repeat, he is not denying an encounter with objects or persons in the world that are independent of us. He is only saying that we cannot know them or speak or write about them or debate about what they are without using language. Objects and persons are not words. They are what they are. But they only exist as what they are for us in our descriptions, in sentences that use a particular language or set of categories. It is a practical matter of what is useful to talk about. Thus he can disavow theory and bid us concentrate on the language games we play. These games involve changes in vocabulary that come into being because someone adopts a new way of speaking because it is believed to be more useful in doing practical things whose consequences can be tested in experience. But we can never experience something (reality) that is not experienced or describe that something without describing it in language. We cannot escape this predicament in which practically speaking reality exists for us only in the language we use.

Nevertheless, difficulties remain. He wants to avoid the Kantian notion of unknown things in themselves. The appearance-reality distinction is not helpful. "Pragmatists — both classical and 'neo' — do not believe that there is a way things really are."[10] Yet he says there were trees, mountains, and giraffes before there were people to refer to them by those names. So what are they in themselves before and apart from human linguistic reference? Did they not exist some way? Were they not what they were in and of themselves totally independent of human perception and description? Was there not a reality in itself prior to the way they appeared to human beings? Saying that things are what they are known as does not mean they are not something existing in some way apart from being known in some particular context. Is there not some reality that is what it is in and of itself that appears to us and is known by us in some way? All I am saying is that in the way they are known to us are clues to what they really are that we can only fallibly, tentatively, and uncertainly interpret, but we can at least do that.

His evolutionary Darwinian epistemology seems to assume that there was a process of evolution actually going on before any human beings came on the scene. So he must either believe that the scientific description of the process has some resemblance to what factually occurred, or his "biologistic" approach collapses. Can we fully dispose of the contrast between the order of reality and the order of knowledge? I do not see how we can escape the reality-appearance distinction despite the fact that it creates all sorts of problems with respect to questions of knowledge, truth, and reality. He goes too far and tries too hard to reduce the true to the useful. A non-useful reductionism results from taking his clue from Darwin and interpreting all human actions as merely more complex ways to cope.

Rorty says that words and languages are just more powerful tools in the struggle to exist and to cope. I say that human beings also seek understanding and to know the truth about things, not just to be successful and to make life better. Beliefs are attempts to say something about the ways things are, not just to provide others clues to what we can be expected to do. He is just wrong when he says, "... when we utter such sentences as 'I am hungry,' we are not making external what was previously external, but are simply helping those around us to predict our future actions."[11] Why can't it be both — an assertion about a state of affairs obtaining within the speaker's body that is real and a clue to future behavior? Human beings seek understanding of how things are and develop plans of action to achieve their purposes. We need to speak of both theory and practice. Surely Whitehead was on to something when he said that practical reason is what Hercules shares with the foxes while theoretical reason is what Plato shares with the gods.[12] Contrary to Rorty, we are a bit more than complicated animals, a dimension neglected in his evolutionary reductionism — his "biologistic view" — that eliminates the search for the true by demoting it totally to the quest for the useful.[13] That "whole brood and nest of dualisms" (Dewey) that he opposes is very hard to get rid of without neglecting something that needs to be taken account of.

I cannot escape the conclusion that he is suspended uncertainly between dissolving reality into the linguistic references we make to it and acknowledging that trees, mountains, and the process of evolution, e.g., have a reality independent of and prior to our speaking of them. The fact that every description of *reality* (which we do not create) is a *description* of reality (which we do create) leads him to dispose too completely of a correspondence theory of reality. There is a way to preserve what is valid in his claims while at the same time preserving a qualified theory of correspondence.

I can make my point by taking up again the statement I used earlier: "The broom is in the closet." Simple observational tests are sufficient to verify or refute claims with regard to statements of this type within the practical context in which they are made. I do not know of anyone, including Rorty, who doubts this, whether they employ a correspondence theory of truth or not. It is not necessary to spell out in detail what I mean, since anyone reading this would know exactly what to do and what tests to apply to determine the truth or falsity of the proposition and would know what correspondence to reality means in this context even if they could not articulate a definition of correspondence that would satisfy Rorty. After the tests have been made, a pronouncement can be made with such absoluteness that we would say of those who disagreed that they did not understand the situation, not that the verdict was open to dispute. The sentence refers to something "out there" existing in a non-linguistic, pre-linguistic mode independent of the minds of those who speak. Its objective reality is not affected by the vocal utterance of those involved. It is something in and of itself. Of course, it is not a "broom" except in the usage of a particular linguistic community using the English language to make the sound or word that stands for whatever it is apart from the human meaning and reality assigned to it.

We are caught in a circularity of words and a web of experiences. The epistemological predicament is that we can never say *what* it is without reference to some background assumptions and some level of what in a broad sense can be called "theory." First of all, there is the word "broom" and its equivalents in other languages. Some languages may not even have an exact or similar word for a thing used to sweep with. One might describe it as a stick with long straws strapped to it, but that does not quite convey the meaning of something used to sweep with for cleaning purposes.[14] Such a simple word has a history in the English language (of which I am totally ignorant!) related to a group of people, their interests in ridding a surface of dirt and dust, succeeding versions of this implement, etc. The use of the term carries with it a nest of assumptions, interests, associations, and the like. Witches ride them, for example.

We learn the word as children without knowing much of the history of the word or the technology. When the question is raised, "Where is the broom?" we know what is meant (once having identified which broom is being spoken of), and we know how to settle the issue of whether it is or is not in the hall closet. Yet it does not make much sense to say that it *is* a "broom" apart from human interests, words, linguistic history, and so on. *What* "that thing there" is in and of itself apart from the human convention of naming it a "broom" is hard to say. But that it is *something* in and of and by itself, most of us will have no doubt. Whatever it is in itself would remain if all human consciousness disappeared. All this obfuscation will not deter a family member needing an implement to sweep out the garage from being quite certain about whether the broom is in the closet in any and every sense that matters to him.[15]

One more step must be taken. Even if we say that the broom is an organization of energy in the spatio-temporal realm constituted as a system of molecular entities, we are merely using the language of another linguistic community, i.e., of modern science. The notion that once we get to the level of elementary particles in physics, we have transcended all of this and are simply in touch with reality as it is in itself is a conceit of the latest claimants to the title of The Special Ones in Possession of Reality and Not Mere Appearance. Rorty makes the same point more effectively than I have. I maintain with him that this is one more interpretation within a certain frame of reference that enables us, among other things, to make useful predictions. I would go on to say that this is made possible by abstracting from the whole of reality and examining it by the methods available to science that yield formulas that can be stated precisely with mathematical exactitude. That particle physics gives us that whole beyond which there is nothing real left to know is exactly what is in dispute, not an obvious certainty. My belief is that science gives us an abstracted perspective on the whole given its means of inquiring, testing, and theorizing but that the concrete entirety requires philosophy as "the critic of abstractions" (Whitehead) to complete the task. Metaphysics, which attempts to define the whole from which all more limited perspectives are abstracted, gives us a perspective that is itself relative to time, place, and interpreter and yields beliefs that cannot be known with certainty to mirror reality, although they may.

Let us note, then, that the "thing" to which the word "broom" refers has other dimensions of reality and other relationships than those immediately in question. Its reality is not exhausted by the way it is known and referred to in the sentence in question. However, in the context in which some speaker uses these words, it is a broom, and the word corresponds, refers to, represents, and points to the reality that is in question. For the moment the other aspects of its reality can be safely ignored but can be focused on as need be for other purposes. Those who use the immediate sentence are in touch with reality, the only reality that matters at that moment. If we ask what the broom is in and of itself independently of being known by us, we are into metaphysics. My own view is that to be real is to have the capacity to affect and to be affected. The total reality of a thing is the sum total of all its effects on and relations to everything else. If we ask further about the nature of those things that can affect and be affected, I am persuaded by a Whiteheadian perspective in which all real things (actual entities) are a set of activities with lifelike qualities, i.e., experiencing subjects. Does this theory about reality correspond with what reality is? Here relativity appears in all its glory. I can only justify this claim with the resources available to me, a perspective dependent on my own historical-cultural location, my life history, and my preferred way of constructing the world. This metaphysical outlook need not be called into play in the immediate situation in which the broom is the reality and the word broom corresponds to it. Beyond that any who care to can debate the metaphysics. Meanwhile, we can settle with absolute finality for all practical purposes for all parties of whatever metaphysical denomination whether the broom is in the closet or not. Within that common sense framework employed in everyday life, the word fully represents the reality, and nothing more need be said. The reality in question is a broom pure and simple.

The reality we call broom is the sum total of all perspectives, relationships, and perceptions in which it stands. At the level at which simple observational tests can verify a claim about the limited dimension of reality that appears to the unaided senses, a correspondence theory is valid. The scientific perspective on this reality (broom) in terms of elementary particles (physics) or molecules (chemistry) is subject to a high degree of verification. However, the debate, between the Kuhnians with their changing paradigms and the realists who think the cumulative process will eventually bring us to a final scientific theory of what the broom and everything else is, is unsettled. As we move into metaphysics and toward theories of ultimate reality, the correspondence theory becomes progressively less serviceable. The disputes that have raged for centuries between the materialists, the idealists, and all the other theories of what the ultimate stuff of the universe really is are not likely ever to reach any final resolution. Here relativity of perspective reigns.

Hence, I mostly agree with Rorty, yet I cannot rid myself of the notion that it is more interesting, more useful, better in some respects to use a different way of speaking. When thinking with our minds, we always and can only speak of an interpreted reality, but prior to conscious thought and independently of it we as bodies in nature encounter the world as it is. If in my sleep while my linguistic practices are idle, a poisonous snake bites me, my body "knows" it. It knows it not as "snake" but responds to something objective in the poison in terms of its own real structures and processes. The poison because of what it is has the power to affect my body in certain ways because of what it is, and the result of this may kill me before my language capacities come into play. Bodily experience gives us clues that we as minds can interpret to make guesses about the reality that we never encounter except as experienced. True, we cannot confront non-experienced, non-interpreted reality as such to test our theories, but we experience data in some part of it that may serve as clues and used as evidence by reason to construct a more workable model of reality as a whole than we had. More workable means successful in bringing more of the world into a coherent interpretive framework while staying close to all relevant evidence and/or proving to be more satisfying by our notion of the good life. All such interpretive schemes are subject to change by imaginative reintegration into a new paradigm.

His recognition of the reality of objects along with his tendency to dissolve the objective reality so totally into the words we use to describe them seems to me an unstable combination. My objective relativism is an attempt to incorporate what is valid in what I have called subjective relativism and objectivism. It is a sharp and dangerous knife edge to be on, but the alternatives so far appear to me to be worse, including the one proposed by Richard Rorty. Is it also an unstable combination, maybe even worse than his? I may be on an unstable boundary between objectivism and relativism, between confidence in reason to discover some patterns inherent in reality and a skepticism and a form of uncertainty that resolves itself in an appeal to what works from me practically.

However, let me make clear just what a modest claim I am making. My insistence on maintaining an objective reference is a need that I have. It is essential for me within my frame of reference to maintain that the uninterpreted world that is what it is independently of us does not tell us what language to use to describe it. However, it gives us clues that we can interpret in the words and concepts that are available to us or that we can invent for the purpose. These interpretations can be tested not only for their usefulness in helping us cope but also in terms of their adequacy to evidence and their coherence with the whole body of ideas we use to understand the world. These interpretations can be revised on the basis of further experience and reflection to become a part of an enlarging body of concepts that we may attempt to integrate more coherently with each other and to gain greater adequacy to experience and evidence.

Such interpretations are tentative, never final, and never fully satisfactory. They are always somebody's interpretation for which certainty as to correct representation to reality can never be claimed. They are matters of faith. Hence, metaphysical and moral systems are best thought of as confessions, to wit: "This is the best I know up to now for all sources. It works for me, and I have no choice but to affirm what I cannot deny." I can only make a personal testimony of the way it seems to me with respect to reason and reality. It is the equivalent of running up a flag to see if anyone salutes. It will be helpful to anyone who finds it useful, true for anyone who finds it true. It can serve practically as a starting point, a way of orientation to the world, a conversational beginning with others to chart agreements and disagreements. It is a basis on which to form alliances with others to sponsor certain ways of believing and acting and to oppose when necessary those who act in ways we find abhorrent or propose policies we deem to be destructive.

Beyond that not much more can be said or need be said. So far as I know, I am the only person living or dead who did or does believe exactly as I do. However, in that I am not alone but only describing a human fact. So all we can do is confess our faith and interact with each other in harmony or conflict as peacefully as possible. What is useless and ought not to be done, in my opinion, is to waste time debating about who really has it right, sees it as God sees it, or is describing the world the way the world would if it knew what it was.[16] In saying all this, it may be that I am so close to Rorty that my efforts to preserve a meaningful reality reference in theories collapse. It could be that I either have to adopt his outlook entirely or develop a more substantive and robust realism than I have done here.

The Trinity of Knowledge
Reality
Experience   Interpretation

Knowing involves an interplay among three factors. Initially, reality means "what is actually the case, objectively there in fact." Experience means "what happens in and to or by the agency of human beings as registered biologically in their bodies and/or perceived, consciously or unconsciously; life as lived and felt." Interpretation means "linguistic description and explanation constituting the theory formation by which the world is constructed and articulated; everything contributed to the knowing process that is not a part of the immediate natural perception of human organisms." Conventionally, it can be put this way:

Objective	**Subjective**
Reality	Experience
	Interpretation

While this type of analysis is altogether conventional and perhaps finally unsustainable, it serves a useful purpose for me. Objective in tendency means here "independent of the subject, determined or at least contributed by the object, what is there, whether experienced or experienceable or not." Subjective is bent toward "occurring within or received, constructed, or otherwise contributed by the experiencer." These distinctions are abstractions from a stream of unified processes useful for analysis but misleading if the mutual dependence and the flowing of each into the others is obscured.[17] Each can serve, on occasion, as a complete epistemological reference by embracing the others. When we see cars moving down the street, watch a loved one die, determine that a disease was caused by a virus, appreciate the beauty of the sunset, confess the goodness of God, etc., alternately we can say:

we are in touch with *reality*;

reality is being *experienced*; or

experienced reality is being *interpreted*.

Conceivably, something may be real that is not knowable by human beings. What counts for us, however, is what is experienced and experienceable, directly or indirectly, now or later. What is experienced matters much, but prior to or apart from interpretation may mean little, except for whatever value attaches to sheer perception, awareness, and sensation as such. An indissoluble connection exists among reality, experience, and interpretation, yet each also has a relative autonomy. Neither can be wholly reduced to the others, nor can they be fully separated except abstractly for purposes of analysis.

We (I do anyway!) have an incontrovertible and ineradicable confidence that we live in a world that is prior to and independent of our experience of it. I believe that events occurred before I was born that my parents have told me about. Similarly, I believe that events are occurring now to other people in other places that I may learn about later. If my consciousness disappeared tomorrow, the universe of such happenings would otherwise still exist. Experience is *of* reality. In the most comprehensive framework that includes all experiencing of all experiencers past, present, and future, experience *is* reality, i.e., the only reality that matters. Yet experience as pure perception or consciousness logically prior to interpretation, while full of content, is relatively low in human meaning. This is certainly the case when compared to the culturally-enriched mode of interpreting experience made possible by historically-created ways of constructing the world. Hence, while I agree with Rorty that it is futile to try to separate out precisely what is contributed to knowledge by the object (the world) and what is contributed buy the subject (the mind), I want to keep objective reality in the picture and struggle with all the difficulties thereunto appertaining.

The human epistemological predicament is that we have no infallible way of accurately separating out these three elements. Nor can we precisely identify what contributes precisely what to our complete inventory of beliefs in each of the relevant spheres in which the question arises (scientific inquiry and religious experience, e.g.). We only know reality as experienced and interpreted. But what is real in and of itself in relation to what we experience? And how does interpretation shape or determine what is real as experienced? We go around and around. All we have is the connectedness of the three. Attempts to define, identify, and locate each in relation to the other are caught up in a circular process that cannot be fully transcended in order to provide a final resolution. No supreme court can be appealed to, since all judges are themselves immersed in the same predicament and circularity. Hence, we can never be sure how successful our efforts are.

The aim is to understand and cope with reality, but our only access to the real is what I call "interprience," i.e., interpreted experience. We know the world as experienced and as interpreted. However, all elucidations of experience transpire within the framework of our inherited language and our accepted cultural traditions as they are embodied concretely in particular elucidators. What we bring linguistically and conceptually to experience partly dictates what we will be able to see before we even look and inevitably shapes it when we do. At the same time, however, experiences new or old may alter the interpretive order. Creative imagination moves back and forth between settled interpretive schemes and fresh perceptions, on the one hand, and between familiar experiences and novel interpretive schemes, on the other hand. We are neither frozen into established ways of explicating experience nor entirely free from them. Hence, while we are constrained by what we have come to believe already, from whatever sources and for whatever reasons, we are not enslaved by this fact. We may, however, have blind spots. Reality as experienced and interpreted — that is what knowledge is all about. The search for truth is an adventure of hope without finalities or absolute certainties.

The Anatomy Of Experience

Experience is not a passive receiving of data from outside. Perception itself is the organism's power of grasping or feeling of its surroundings for the sake of promoting the art of living. Experience is the active engagement of a living subject with the environment. It is first of all an emotional affair — terrifying and fascinating, pleasurable and painful, threatening and promising, enjoyable and ecstatic, dull and boring, dreadful and miserable. Experiencers have intentions, interests, and goals. They initiate purposive action and respond to objects and the initiatives of other subjects. Knowing, feeling, and choosing are ingredients in the commerce of experiencing agents with what is real, i.e., with what has power to affect them. Subjects engage the world to overcome obstacles, solve problems, and to achieve ends, as well as to understand it.

Experiencing is in the most comprehensive sense but another name for living. It is the inner, subjective reality of the comprehensive process that is life. Knowing facilitates the thoroughly practical affair of living as a process of actualizing the potential for enjoyment given with the gift of life. Even contemplation is not a purely disinterested entertainment of realities and possibilities without practical consequence but an enjoyment that contributes to fullness of life. Knowing in human beings is continuous with that practical engagement with the world that makes up the experience of animals rooted in instinct, habit, innate intelligence, and learned savvy.

Briefly, the underlying cosmology that supports these views is that nature is one complex flux of lifelike events all taking account of (experiencing, prehending, responding to, having a perspective on) each other in a dynamic, ordered, but not fully harmonious whole. Human beings are members of this community of perceivers uniquely gifted in taking account of, and in developing linguistically sophisticated perspectives on, their surroundings.

Pragmatism And Realism

Throughout this chapter I recognize the partial legitimacy of both pragmatic and realist interpretations of truth. On the one hand, in the knowing process the final reference is always to experience and to its interpretation. More precisely, truth ultimately has to do with the relationships between some ideas, other ideas, and the sum total of experiences. To say that something is real amounts to the claim that competent experiencers have had, are now having, or could have certain ideas or experiences. Whatever is real (that matters) can affect us in some way. As William James was fond of saying, reality is what it is "known as."[18] The crucial question is what practical difference it makes in our experience whether we hold one belief or another. If no practical experienceable difference ever arises from affirming A rather than B, the dispute is futile, a waste of time, irrelevant, even meaningless. Truth is the so far verified or well-established in quest of the potentially verifiable, where satisfactory workability in the totality of experience is the final test of all claims.

On the other hand, reality is prior to our experience of it. Reality is determinative in some sense of our experiences. To some degree reality is manifest in and to experience. This implies that the content, the sequences, the connections, and the entire pattern of relationships that constitute our experiences detect and reflect what is going on in the world itself. The reason we *experience* water boiling minutes after it is put on a hot stove is that a causal connectedness inheres in *reality* that is determinative of our perceptions. The reason I *feel pain* when I place my finger too close is that *the stove is hot*. Hence, truth is not first of all about me — my ideas and my perceptions — but about the world. Experience is *of reality*. We experience things a certain way because the order of nature is a certain way. Hence, reality is antecedent to and independent of our experiences and our interpretations of it. Truth is description adequate to realities, an account of how things really are or can reasonably be believed to be, not merely a survey of what practically works for us.

The pragmatist in me latches onto the fact that reality for us is what we know it to be and thus forgoes any reality claims that are not, in some sense, experience claims. The realist in me locks onto the priority and independence of reality in relation to experience. Depending on which of these perspectives becomes the organizing center, a pragmatist or a realist interpretation may follow. Each perspective is partially valid but incomplete without the other.[19] In ordinary language within relatively simple circumstances, a correspondence theory of truth works quite well, if we say precisely what we mean by it. But what is it that corresponds to what? Within certain limited frameworks it will suffice to say that the correspondence is between the words and the world. More precisely, it is an agreement between certain ideas, words, meanings, and descriptions, on the one hand, and certain experiences of the intended object.

Justification of belief takes on many meanings with differing possibilities of achieving assent depending on the claim being made. Universal assent on ultimate matters of fact is no guarantee of truth that corresponds to reality. At some point, we begin to deal with claims about matters of fact whose truth is not certain, allowing only for varying degrees of adequacy for understanding and coping, depending on the context. Yet even theories about God that cannot be verified with certainty may have important consequences for living. In agreement with William James that differences that make no difference in life now or later do not matter, we may safely ignore those that do not.[20] Theoretical and pragmatic considerations are relevant to the testing of theological claims. Based on prior learnings and theories, present beliefs are in part tested by the consequences of living as if they were true. What we seek is a way of intelligent practice based on theories that both satisfactorily interpret and unify our experience and that teach us how to come to want and to get what we would want if we fully understood the ends and obligations that maximize happiness under conditions of justice. This does not mean that religious beliefs should not be tested theoretically in terms of their appropriateness to our best interpretations of reality. It only means that all such validation is internal to the point of view being verified and thus relative and perspectival. The appeal may be to public evidence and criteria in principle available to all, but all judgments thus derived reflect particular readings of the situation.[21]

Revision Of An Old Story

A little story can bring this to a close. If I understand Rorty, he is saying something like this:

Okay, mountains, trees, and giraffes existed before anyone ever called them that. Yes, a process of evolution did really go on before human beings came along. The point is that it simply is useless and a waste of time to pursue the question as to what mountains, giraffes, and evolution are in themselves apart from our talking about them since that gets us back into all those irresolvable disputes about reality in contrast to appearance. Let us just stick to what we can deal with in ways that have some practical benefit. We cannot know what reality is apart from our descriptions of it. The true is the useful.

The following is a rewriting of an old joke. In the original story a man was looking for something in a pile of junk illuminated by a nearby lamppost. When someone came along and inquired, he replied that he was looking for the keys to his car. When further queried, he admitted that he lost the keys in the huge vacant lot across the street, but it was useless to look for them over there because it was too dark. In my version Rorty is the searcher. I offer to help him and go over into the pitch black area with a lot of stuff lying around. Rorty is under the lamppost finding some interesting things now and then but no car keys. He uses whatever he finds for whatever practical purpose it may serve and is willing to leave it at that. I am over in the dark vacant lot finding a lot of items and occasionally something that feels like a key. I speculate about the car it might fit. When I checked with him once, he told me that actually his car had been stolen and shipped overseas but that he didn't really care, although he once did.[22] He had given up the hopeless search for the car keys, but he was having so much fun with all the useful stuff he was finding he didn't miss the lost car anymore. But he is sure that my search for the keys to the real car is worthless. We both agree that we can never locate the car itself to make a definitive test as to whether any of the keys I am finding will go in the keyhole of the car and crank it up. So Rorty is content to use whatever he finds in the junk whenever it will do something helpful for him, throwing away some things when more useful stuff is found. I keep thinking that this car is somewhere, and one of these keys I am finding might just fit. Anyway, I keep wondering about it and puzzling over it. Rorty thinks I am wasting my time and that I would be happier if I got out of the dark and joined him in the light. Like him I could use whatever I find whenever it comes in handy. Perhaps I should take his advice, but I cannot bring myself to abandon the quest. I sure wish I could see that car and get in it and see if any of the keys I have found will make it run. So who is the idiot in this story? Maybe both of us are. Maybe neither of us is. But we don't know how to answer that question either.

In the next chapter I will examine some prominent ways philosophers and theologians have employed to acquire moral truth and set forth my own peculiar views on the subject.

Endnotes

1. See Richard Rorty, *Philosophy and the Mirror of Nature* (Princeton: Princeton University Press, 1979); *Consequences of Pragmatism* (Minneapolis: University of Minnesota Press, 1982); and *Contingency, Irony, and Solidarity* (Cambridge: Cambridge University Press, 1989).

2. When he is accused of relativism, Rorty says, "So ... when the pragmatist says that there is nothing to be said about truth save that each of us will commend as true those beliefs which he or she finds good to believe, the realist is inclined to interpret this as one more positive theory about the nature of truth. But the pragmatist does not have a theory of truth, much less a relativistic one.... [H]is account of the value of cooperative human inquiry has only an ethical base, not an epistemological or metaphysical one. Not having any epistemology, *a fortiori* he does not have a relativistic one." "Relativism" (The Howison Lecture delivered at the University of California, Berkeley, January 31, 1983), 8f. While this reply may be valid from Rorty's

point of view, the objectivist or realist is also correct in calling Rorty a relativist from their point of view.

3. "To say that we should drop the idea of truth as out there waiting to be discovered is not to say that we have discovered that, out there, there is no truth. It is to say that our purposes would be served best by ceasing to see truth as a deep matter, as a topic of philosophical interest, or 'true' as a term which repays 'analysis.'" Richard Rorty, *Contingency, Irony, and Solidarity*, 8.

4. Richard Rorty, *Achieving Our Country: Leftist Thought in Twentieth-Century America* (Cambridge: Harvard University Press, 1998).

5. Cf. this exchange between Richard J. Bernstein and Rorty. Bernstein says, "If we accept Rorty's claim that all justification, whether of knowledge or moral choices, cannot hope to escape from history and only makes sense with reference to social practices, we are still faced with the critical task of determining which social practices are relevant, which ones ought to prevail, be modified, or abandoned." *Philosophical Profiles: Essays in a Pragmatic Mode* (Philadelphia: University of Pennsylvania Press, 1986). Rorty replies that just because we recognize that our truths and our moral values are contingent, that does not mean, despite this irony, that they are not worthy of commitment because of their lack of metaphysical anchorage. See *Contingency, Irony, and Solidarity*, 6.

6. Foundationalism is the view that we can locate by reason or somewhere in experience a foundation that is indubitable on the basis of which we can come to know more about reality.

7. Cf. Donald Davidson, "Where we differ, if we do, is on whether there remains a question how, given that we cannot 'get outside our beliefs and our language so as to find some test other than coherence,' we nevertheless can have knowledge of, and talk about, an objective public world which is not of our own making. I think this question does remain, while I suspect that Rorty doesn't think so." "A Coherence Theory of Truth and Knowledge," in *Reading Rorty* (Oxford: Basil Blackwell, 1990).

8. Donald Davidson, "On the Very Idea of a Conceptual Scheme," in *Inquiries into Truth and Representation* (Oxford: at the Clarendon Press, 1984), 183-98. So far as I can tell in the end Davidson only wants to change the way we speak about truth, objectivity, words, sentences, and correspondence. Words and sentences still have some connection with the world, with experience. He wants to insist that truth has to do not with correspondence to reality but to the relation between speakers and their sentences about the world. Truth

may hold between propositions that assert fact about the world or experience, but is not grounded in correspondence with this reality. Involved in this is his conviction that we cannot speak of an uninterpreted reality to which we can compare our words and sentences to see if they correspond — a sentiment I accept. What he wants is not truth relative to conceptual schemes but truth of sentences relative to language. Nevertheless, he says, "We do not give up the world but reestablish unmediated touch with the familiar objects whose antics make our sentences and opinions true and false." 198. "Unmediated touch with familiar objects" is what I contend for in my own way.

9. I suspect many would agree with me that when they speak of different conceptual schemes, they mean that ways of thinking differ in background assumptions, method, and content, not taking into consideration at the moment whether one is fully translatable into another or not. Davidson denies the distinction between conceptual scheme and its content. He may be right if the assumption is that scheme and content are independent of each other or that they can be completely separated. However, it may be better to think of the conceptual scheme not as something independent of the content but as the total pattern of thought implicit in the content containing the background assumptions and framework that are essential to the meaning of the content, that ground it, and without which particular assertions would lack support and collapse. The conceptual scheme is not separate from the content but is the structural whole implicit within and necessary to the particular statements that constitute the content and that gives it cogency. When Aquinas offers a cosmological argument for the existence of God and Kant refutes it, they bring to their claims assumptions, presuppositions, and background theories about epistemology and metaphysics that I am calling the structural whole, the total pattern implicit in the content of their arguments that makes them meaningful and convincing from each point of view. So in this sense we can make a distinction between scheme and content, but they are not separate or independent, but the former is the whole ensemble of assumed postulates essential to the meaning and persuasiveness of the latter and implicit within it. Whether scientific talk about quarks and electrons can be translated into every other language on earth past and present, I do not know. But I doubt that it can be made meaningful unless the background premises that constitute the structural whole within which talk about these particular entities takes place is also translated and conveyed to users of other languages along with statements about quarks and electrons. I am suggesting that conceptual scheme can be used to refer to the background assumptions that constitute the structural whole within which talk about quarks and electrons — the content — takes place and without which it would make no sense.

10. Richard Rorty, *Philosophy and Social Hope* (London: Penguin Books, 1999), 27.

11. *Ibid.,* xxiv.

12. Alfred North Whitehead, *The Function of Reason* (Boston: Beacon Press, 1958), 10.

13. I would agree with him that "everything we say and do and believe is a matter of fulfilling human needs and interests" if only he would include the need to understand for its own sake as one of those needs and interests. *Ibid.,* xxvii.

14. Just out of curiosity, I reached for my dictionary and looked up the word. The first meaning is: "a sweeping implement consisting of a brush of twigs or plant stems on a handle." *The American College Dictionary* (1949).

15. For a more detailed discussion with even more obfuscation, see my *Theological Biology,* 78-83, from which portions of the preceding discussion were taken.

16. We can discuss with each other why we prefer our own schemes, give reasons for our preferences and against opposing views. Even when we pronounce another wrong, it is always understood to mean wrong from my perspective.

17. In this way I believe I avoid what Wilfred Sellars calls "the myth of the Given," an empirical foundation in something objective on which reliable knowledge of the world can rest secure. I insist on the interdependence of reality, experience, and interpretation and maintain that we cannot separate them clearly and infallibly from each other. All we have is the togetherness of the three. See Wilfred Sellars, "Empiricism and the Philosophy of Mind," *Minnesota Studies in the Philosophy of Science 1,* Hebert Feigl and Michael Scriven, eds. (Minneapolis: University of Minnesota Press, 1956).

18. William James, *Pragmatism* (New York: Meridian Books, 1955), 45. He attributed the phrase to Shadworth Hodgson.

19. Cf. *ibid.,* pp. 198-9.

20. William James, *Pragmatism,* 44-5.

21. Theology has many dimensions. I focus here on the reality claims made by theological propositions. The total task of theology also involves interpretation of texts, historical inquiry, making prescriptions for living, working, and worshiping (applying religious truth to life), and so on. Each of these tasks has its own aims, procedures, and criteria of truth and adequacy.

22. To make this part of the story a bit more plausible, it might be noted that Rorty spent the years between fifteen and twenty years of age trying to be a Platonist, searching for a comprehensive theory that would "hold reality and justice in a single vision" (Yeats). *Philosophy and Social Hope,* 7-9.

Chapter 4

How Can We Acquire Moral Truth? Three Answers

How do we acquire moral truth? Three widely employed approaches are natural law, human reason, and divine revelation. Supporters maintain that their preferred method can provide moral norms that are universally valid and objectively true. I shall argue that they provide no path to certain truth but only to perspectives that can be justified only by a set of presuppositions internal to themselves. This does not necessarily mean that they do not offer us universal truth that is objectively valid but only that their methods provide no guarantee of having done so.

Natural Law

The natural law tradition has a long and distinguished history.[1] Its central claim is that moral norms are built into the fundamental structure of the world (nature) and that reason can discern its patterns (law). Its main virtue lies in the quest for objectivity and universality in ethical theory. Its primary limitation is that any statement of natural law is relative to the time, place, culture, and outlook of its formulators. Hence, the quest for objectivity and universality is called into question. Despite this, merit attaches to the effort to seek agreement about moral norms based on principles that are potentially available to all rational inquirers. The appeal to reason rather than to traditions peculiar to particular cultures or religions is the basis of its enduring appeal. Yet reason is not the impartial "spectator of all time and existence" (Plato) but the instrument of finite reasoners whose insights are shaped by the specific intellectual resources available to them in their culture and their own inventory of rational tools. They will employ the language, category system, factual beliefs, value commitments, and general assumptions about the world, human beings, and ultimate reality known to them. The notion that a philosopher's mind is a mirror in which natural law is reflected will not bear examination. If any clouding by the cultural medium is admitted, then the project is spoiled, since we have no way of knowing what is adulterated and what is pure. No supreme court is available to adjudicate disputes since any arbiter to whom appeal might be made or who claims superior wisdom is subject to the same limitations as the original disputants. All reason is historical — the instrument of time- and culture-bound communities and individuals. Nevertheless, this does not foreclose the possibility that from some specific stance a grasp of the objective moral order can be known in whole or part. The troubling issue always is knowing whether such an order actually exists and when we have accurately discerned its features.

The liabilities of natural law theory are well-known. First of all, natural law has been claimed in the past as the justification for practices that nearly everyone now recognizes as evil. Slavery and the denial of the right to vote to women are obvious examples. In the second place, competent interpreters in the past and present have disagreed about what natural law mandates. A century and a half ago slaveholders and abolitionists alike claimed natural law as the basis of their contrary claims. Today a dispute rages about whether same-sex love is morally offensive because it is "unnatural." Finally, natural law is distorted by self-interest. This refers not only to renderings clearly dictated by selfish bias but also to the slant given to things by all our loves and loyalties. We need not think that the slaveholders and the intellectuals who provided them with pro-slavery arguments were perfidious or insincere in thinking that nature or God justified the ownership of Africans by whoever could afford to buy them. Men in the nineteenth century may have honestly believed that nature taught that woman's place was in the home. Nevertheless, we are justified in questioning in both cases whether the fact that their interpretation of natural law benefitted them was just a happy coincidence or in part a distortion of thought rooted in self-interest.

If we agree that great minds have been egregiously wrong about the principles of natural law in the past, what gives us confidence that our present readings that seem so convincing to us are right? Serious moralists, of course, have some limited ability to recognize their own bias and self-interest. Honest seekers of truth can to some extent transcend their own parochialism in quest of a more impartial outlook but not in such a way as to overcome the fundamental relativity that makes it impossible to rise above the resources available to us at a given time and cultural location.

Natural law has no advantage that is not obtained by the simple claim that we affirm and commit ourselves to act upon the best we know up to now from all sources. Moreover, we seek the agreement of other morally-serious agents in support of the principles and norms that command our allegiance. We remain in conversation with those who oppose us and stay open to further insight as a consequence of this engagement. The content of belief and the agreement that can be secured with others is the crucial point. It is not essential to get agreement that our convictions are reports of discoveries we have made by examining a moral law built into reality itself. It is useful, however, for all parties to state the reasons for believing what they do and to recite the history and the experience that led to these convictions and to the inescapable and undeniable status they now have in their minds and hearts — at least for now. We can engage each other as historical beings whose beliefs are relative to our time and place and confess to each other how and why we came to believe as we do while being open to learn and to change as the consequence of our encounters. But we add nothing to content or to commitment by arguing over whether we ought to base our convictions on natural law.

It is, of course, legitimate and helpful for proponents of natural law to explain how they go about the task of reasoning about morality. But should we all do our ethics that way? Suppose two people agree that a principle of social ethics is that society ought to maximize liberty, equality, and the common good consistent with the constraint each of these mandates puts on the others.[2] One party declares this to be a principle of natural law known to reason. The other party thinks reason is too infected with finitude and sin to be a reliable guide but affirms the stated principle to be an implication of biblical revelation. For explanatory, confessional, and comparative purposes, each might usefully elucidate the rationale for preferring reason or revelation as the source of moral truth. But the fact that they agree on the principle is the crucial point, not how they arrive at it. They would do well to work together to achieve the ideal in some actual society and to spend little time arguing over whether natural law is a legitimate basis for it or only divine self-disclosure. And will they not jointly oppose those with contrary views whether their opponents claim revelation or reason or both as their authorization?

What do the proponents of natural law do when confronted with other competent and honest seekers of the law of nature who stubbornly disagree with them? No satisfactory resolution of this problem is available that does not weaken the claims made about natural law. What are the options? (1) One can pronounce opponents to be just plain wrong. The spectacle of two absolutists declaring each other to be in error is not edifying. What is the practical point of maintaining the objectivity and universality of natural law known by reason if we cannot agree on its content? One might reply that we contend with each other in order to come to a better understanding of it. But how do we know when we have? The best we can say is that once we believed A but now we believe B and give the reasons we changed our minds. The premises of natural law theory lead us to expect that it yields true belief, but it offers no way for us to know for sure that we have achieved it. (2) One can relativize all claims about the content of natural law. But to the extent that one does, the claims to universality and objectivity are vitiated. (3) They can speak of relative adequacy based on "a consensus of warranted affirmations."[3] This is an improvement, but in some respects it merely shifts the terms of the debate without resolving the relativity issues. It leaves still to be resolved what constitutes a consensus in what community. When are affirmations warranted, and who decides? In all three cases the disputants can engage each other with indeterminate possibilities that one will convert the other or that both will undergo a change of mind leading toward consensus. This is well and good, and such debates ought to occur with mutual respect and openness to genuine conversion. But the agreement that is or is not achieved is the decisive practical point, not the claim that the norms we espouse are grounded in natural law.

My critique is not centered in the outright, unqualified denial either (1) of the reality of natural law as such or (2) of the correctness of claims about its content in particular instances but in skepticism about the capacity of reason to possess such knowledge with certainty. Hence, the problem lies not so much in the fact that reason can never grasp universal, objective principles embedded in the structure of reality itself but in knowing for sure whether it can and when it has done so. Since we cannot have indisputable knowledge either that reason has the general capacity to discern the law of nature or that we have correctly read its features in particular cases, we are left in the predicament of not knowing for sure whether we are dealing with knowledge or with belief. The stubborn fact of history is that in practical terms we have a plurality of contending parties who must decide what they will do with each other. The worthwhile task is to seek agreement where possible and to forego definitive resolution of the theoretical impasse between the absolutists and the relativists. This dilemma calls for a different approach to the whole problem. My suggestion is that we simply set forth our own beliefs and the justification for them as confessions of belief regarding how it seems to us from where we stand. If someone wants to maintain that these beliefs are rooted in natural law, well and good. I and others can only evaluate such a claim on the basis of our own beliefs.

I can affirm my sincere conviction that mechanical or chemical means of birth control are morally permissible. What I cannot do is to say for sure that this belief corresponds with a pattern existing in the structure of reality itself. The line between belief and knowledge cannot be crossed with certainty on such matters. Debates between orthodox Roman Catholics and liberal Protestants are resolvable only in the minds of the respective interpreters making use of the principles that for them justify such assertions. We should always give the best reasons we can for what we believe. Moreover, we can and must act as if our beliefs were true when important issues are at stake. We can do so in humility with all appropriate fervor and with effective actions proportional to the importance of the question in dispute.

Hence, my skepticism and relativism lead me to set aside the question of objective validity in moral debates since the issue is not resolvable in theoretical terms. I fall back on a pragmatism that claims only that my views are in conformity with the best available interpretations of morality available to me. They are useful in guiding my choices toward satisfactory outcomes as I judge them. Moreover, I am ever open to changes dictated by future experimental testing and further reflection. Theoretical debates about natural law are not resolvable. Centuries of experience should teach us this. Hence, I seek theories and practices that deal practically with the fact of agreement and disagreement among moralists.

Let each party confess as historical beings whose views are relative to time and place how they came to believe as they do. Let them offer justification of their convictions from within their own reasoning stance. Let them engage in critical dialogue with mutual respect and openness to being converted by the other. Beyond that let the contending factions form alliances with those who agree with them and engage in the good fight for justice. Let them oppose their enemies in all appropriate ways, respecting their humanity while resisting their beliefs and their practices in every relevant arena of human activity, including politics.

It is of very little practical use to engage in theoretical arguments over which views, if any, are in harmony with the law of nature, the will of God, or the structure of reality. As a confessional stance, natural law is a legitimate way to interpret the foundation and content of moral ideals and obligations. This tradition is needed to counter the kind of relativism, skepticism, and pragmatism I espouse. The natural law tradition should be nourished and defended. But its claims to universality and objectivity flounder on the rocks of historical relativity. It exists as one of a plurality of paths to truth, goodness, and beauty. The fact of unconquerable diversity in moral belief and practice leaves us with the urgent and inescapable practical problem of believing what we cannot deny while respecting and yet opposing those who think us to be in error and a threat to the common good. At the same time we can rejoice in the agreement that does exist and join with those who carry the same banners in the arduous task of making real our shared vision of justice and the good life for all.

My skepticism about the natural law tradition rests on the lack of certainty about the content of moral truth. At least I am skeptical of any alleged certainty. Do I know for sure that my skepticism is warranted? No, of course not. Is my relativism, however, self-contradictory? It might be if I asserted that relativism is a universally valid objective truth known with certainty to be so. I make no such claim about this any more than I make such a claim about the invalidity of natural law. I do not deny that some moral claims may indeed represent the objective moral order. The point is that all these questions are unresolvable except in somebody's mind. Absoluteness of subjective confidence in a belief is, of course, no guarantee that it corresponds to reality. Skepticism is no proof that it does not.

This inability to cross the line between subjective belief and objective knowledge defines the human predicament in relation to morality and religion. This does not mean that moral outlooks cannot be tested or that reasoning about them is impossible or useless. It only means that all testing and reasoning take place within a specific framework of assumptions that are historically and culturally relative. I test a moral claim by asking whether it is in harmony with all the rest that I believe and by whether it promotes the well-being of living beings, especially people, and honors their intrinsic worth. However, the most I and others can say is that we are presently unavoidably convinced of our beliefs and will act upon them and oppose contrary views and actions in every way that is appropriate and proportional to the seriousness of the issue at hand. This kind of skepticism, relativism, and pragmatism need not in any way undermine strength of commitment or the courage and capacity to act passionately in accordance with convictions.

Truths Of Reason

Another approach to objectivity and universality in ethics is provided by those who may not refer to natural law but speak more generally of truths of reason. This way is metaphysically timid in that it does not necessarily connect itself with some theory about reality or an objective realm that yields to reason its treasures of moral truth. It simply talks about what people fully informed and free from bias will discover by the correct employment of reason. Moral truth is justified as objective and universal if reason is convinced of the matter, especially if a consensus is achieved or can be hoped for eventually. I will illustrate the point with three contemporary thinkers who each make the case. The first two are taken from two well-known textbooks.

James Rachels

James Rachels distinguishes between two polar extremes regarding moral truth:
1. There are moral facts in the same way that there are facts about stars and planets or else.
2. Our "values" are nothing more than the expression of our subjective feelings.

Rachels rejects the view that moral beliefs must either have the same objective status as facts and theories about natural objects as studied by science or have a purely subjective status in terms of the feelings of groups or individuals and have no validity beyond that. He thinks a third option is the correct one.

3. Moral truths are truths of reason; that is, a moral judgment is true if it is backed by better reasons than the alternatives.[4]

A truth of ethics has reason on its side. It is valid independently of what we feel, prefer, or want. It is more than opinion. If reason requires a moral belief, we are justified in saying that it is true, objective, and universally valid.

The problem with this means of verification is knowing what are the better reasons. This is what moral disputes are often about. Each party claims to have made the best case on rational grounds. Both sides of the abortion debate claim to be reasoning correctly. The issue here is not whether we should appeal to reason rather than to feelings, preferences, custom, divine revelation, or anything else. The disputants do not agree on what reason requires. How will we decide rationally between Rawls and Nozick regarding the weight to be given to freedom and to equality when it comes to the distribution of social goods? These two philosophers simply have different priorities, and reason cannot resolve the issue definitively. Only people using their reason can assign weight to competing values, although in many cases we might achieve unanimity or come close to it. Rachels bypasses the fact that reason is always somebody's reason. Judgments are not made by some universal faculty the same everywhere and in everybody that we call reason. They are made by reasoners who reason on the basis of certain assumptions dependent on their location in some historical time and cultural place or to some individual idiosyncrasy. Equally rational, equally well-informed philosophers sincerely seeking the truth may simply have different value preferences.[5]

His view that right is what has the best reasons to support it merely shifts the terms of the debate. Arguing about which view has the stronger reasons has all the same problems as feuding about which view most adequately represents reality. Another question is whether the highest morality is identical with what reason would suggest. Reinhold Niebuhr argues that mutual love is the highest rational standard but that Christian ethics is centered in sacrificial love. Is it rational to sacrifice one's own just interest for another out of love? Or is there a transrational dimension here that defies reason? Niebuhr argues that *agape* is not totally reasonable but requires a transhistorical grounding in faith. He means that it cannot validate itself in history with all its tragedy, irrationality, and injustice rooted in egocentrism. If *agape* is not rationally justifiable in this life, does that invalidate it?[6] Equally reasonable people may differ. The point is that the identity of rationality and morality is not self-evident or beyond dispute. Christians can argue that for them morality is based on the will of God, not reason.

In order to argue that morality has a standard independent of the will of God, Rachels makes a false dichotomy. To say that God wills the right because it is right — to avoid divine arbitrariness that could conflict with divine goodness — does not mean that right has a standard independent of God's will. It can mean that the right is simply part of God's own nature or structure and therefore internal to God. It need not be thought of as existing outside God so that God must consult it just as we do to learn what is right. Rather, we may assume an internal harmony and unity within God so that God does not and cannot will in an arbitrary fashion but neither has to consult an independent standard in order to know the right and the good. God only needs to will in harmony with the divine nature.[7] Hence, it may be that to ask what God wills and what is the right thing to do will lead to the same answer but not because God and we are consulting the same standard independent of us and of God. Asking about the right is the same as asking what God's character or nature requires — given the Christian understanding of God as I understand it. In that sense there is no standard of right independent of God. Whether the will of God can be known by reason unaided by divine self-disclosure is another issue.

Finally, does he assume that the rational is the universally agreed upon, or can the lone dissenter actually give the better reasons and therefore be right? If universal assent is not the final test of superior reasoning, what is? If he cannot specify whose judgments about the stronger reasons are decisive, he leaves us right in the middle of the debates about right and wrong where we started. Neither a simple appeal to reason nor to consensus is of much use in settling moral disputes. I argue that the plurality of views results not only because some opinions rest on less than the best reasons but other factors as well. These factors include the fact that actual reason as it operates in history is infected with historical and cultural relativity and corrupted by prejudice and self-interest. Reason decides nothing important about right and wrong. Only reasoners do.

Rachels attempts to overcome relativism by insisting that all cultures agree on a few basic moral rules that are necessary for the existence of society, such as the prohibition against murder, lying, and the care of children. It might seem that the practice of infanticide among Eskimos is an exception with respect to the care of the young, but Rachels argues that it is not. Infanticide was a desperate, last-ditch measure necessary to ensure the survival of the rest of the family under severe environmental conditions marked by scarcity of resources. Presumably if material resources were plentiful and birth control methods were available, they would love their children and keep them alive just as we do. His point here is convincing if that is the total explanation, and I have no reason to doubt that it is. Even if a few basic moral principles are common to all cultures, however, this does not resolve the issue of relativism with respect to the many important issues on which there is no universal agreement even within our own society. Appealing to reason to settle disputes settles nothing. Moreover, truths of reason finally means nothing more than a consensus or unanimity of subjective agreement. Thus he seems to be close to the next thinker.

William Frankena

William Frankena shifts attention from reason as such to agreement among competent interpreters. Says he, "... we may say that a basic moral judgment, principle, or code is justified or 'true' if it is or will be agreed to by everyone who takes the moral point of view and is clearheaded and logical and knows all that is relevant about himself, mankind, and the universe."[8] He does not assume that his own normative principles of beneficence and justice have been proven, but it may be hoped that others may concur when attempting the same thing. Individual thinkers are not obligated to bow to any present majority. No present consensus is final. The precise claim is that a true belief will be consented to ultimately by all who think clearly, are fully informed, and who assume a moral stance. This day may not come until the Day of Judgment. No one can claim full justification now. The appeal is to an ultimate or eschatological consensus. The true or right is what will finally be agreed to by all when all the facts are known and all barriers to right thinking have been cleared away, a day that may never actually come. This is an ideal consensus beyond all current societies and majorities.

Frankena has the advantage over Rachels in that universal agreement is a more useful standard than reason itself as a criterion of objective validity in that it has an empirical referent, at least ultimately and ideally. Let us leave aside the fact that even if an ideal rationality ultimately achieves unanimity, it still requires an act of faith to bridge the gap between universal consent and objective truth (correspondence to reality). Frankena bypasses that issue. He simply defines truth as that which commands universal consent. That is the end of the matter. The practical fact is, of course, that agreement is the best we can hope for. If we all agree, that is as far as we can go at any given moment. Moreover, we can know when we have achieved it. We no longer debate the morality of slavery or whether women should vote since a consensus has been achieved.

The problem, however, is that the remote possibility of eschatological consensus does not help us right now on those issues in which conflict reigns in our own society. We are offered a formal standard of judgment whose material and specific content is not known in the present but only "in the end — which never comes or comes only at the Day of Judgment."[9] Even if a consensus on some issue emerges at some point, it is possible that the ultimate unanimity will overthrow it, so that dissenters can still hope and argue that in the end, they will be vindicated. All parties can maintain that ultimately their position will be sustained against that of all rivals. In the meantime, disputes go on unresolved and unresolvable. But here and now is when we need resolution. When the answers are known, they will be of no value to those who have died long before the ideal rational community renders its ultimate verdict that commands the assent of all competent rational agents. Frankena at least offers us a sure way of testing — if only it were available to us here and now when we need it.

In his refutation of relativism Frankena makes a distinction between basic ethical beliefs and derivative ones — the same procedure used by Rachels. It amounts to recognizing the importance of the context. He notes that in some societies children believe they should kill their parents before they get old. They think they will be better off in the hereafter if they enter before they are debilitated. They share a belief with us, however, that children should do the best they can for their parents. Their belief in killing parents is derived from this basic value, so that the difference between them and us is a factual one and not a matter of having different fundamental values. This is an interesting distinction and useful in reminding us to take the context of moral belief into account. However, his solution, like that of Rachels, does not help us with all those issues about which there is disagreement about basics. Here his only recourse is to eschatology — the Last Day in which all will finally see the light.

In some ways Rachels' example of the Eskimos is better for the purpose than that of Frankena. Presumably, Eskimos moving to the United States who prospered would not kill their children for lack of resources to care for them. But suppose some members of Frankena's society immigrated to this country and retained their belief in the afterlife, would he agree that they should be permitted to kill their parents under the First Amendment right to freedom of religion? After all, they have the same basic family values that Americans do. They just have a strange belief about what happens when we die. Either he has to permit them this religious practice, persuade them to abandon their views of what happens after death, or admit that the distinction between basic and derivative values is of not much practical value in this case. He could maintain that they should be prevented from this practice since if they want to live in our society, they must abide by our laws. Of course, if we start qualifying everybody's beliefs so that we all become more like each other, obviously we come closer to a consensus. I do not know how a world conference of anthropologists and philosophers would settle the question as to how far cultures of the world agree on basics and differ only in derivatives. Would it matter practically at the moment?

Some apologists for slavery argued that the practice was best for everybody including slaves. Do they agree basically with abolitionists that we should do what is best for everybody and differ only in derivative beliefs about whether slavery meets that standard? Of course, he could argue that slavery actually confirms his point, since we all agree now that freedom for all is better than bondage for some. Hence, we may hope that over the long run, we may reach consensus on many other, if not all, moral questions. But this eschatological prospect does little to help us with the relativism and diversity that now prevails and will for the foreseeable future.

Frankena's position rests on the confidence that there is a universal rationality transcending all particular perspectives that may be or could be manifest in a consensus of ideal thinking. Is there? That is what the argument is about. That there is, at the moment, is a faith and a hope. He may be right, but until the universal consensus is actually achieved, we deal in history with stubborn differences that reflect the historical and cultural location of interpreters of morality, along with their peculiar life experiences and personal philosophies. His universalism and my relativism are unproven, but until universalism is achieved, relativism prevails in fact, and that is what matters practically at the moment.

Jürgen Habermas

Jürgen Habermas, like Frankena, adopts the pragmatic standard of truth proposed by James Sanders Peirce — whatever an ideal rational community would ultimately agree to. The aim of Habermas is to sustain the Enlightenment project of political emancipation and democracy. Assuming freedom and reason as the gifts of all individuals, however diverse their backgrounds and cultures, he proposes a method and standard for attaining universality that overcomes relativism. Autonomy and rationality enable humanity to be the author of governing law. Discourse ethics requires a community of free and equal citizens who engage in conversation in order to arrive at the conditions under which they will agree to live together and cooperate. Lifting the "veil of ignorance" and abandoning the individualism assumed by Rawls, he proposes that participants come with all their particular interests and conceptions of the good in full awareness of the perspectives and interpretations of others. Everyone may question any assertion, introduce any proposal, and express any attitude, desire, or need. For this process to work, certain ideal conditions must be presupposed. All must stand in solidarity, showing concern for others and the well-being of the society as a whole. Everyone must respect the rights of all others as free, autonomous rational agents. All must be freed from any deep systematic distortions of thought, prejudices, dogmatic ideologies, oppressive power, or other influences that inhibit the capacity to engage in free, open-minded rational discourse. The hope is that in such a democratic setting under "ideal speech" conditions consent will be evoked by the "unforced force of the better argument." Basic policies are validated or justified by rational agreement on the part of all in a way that gives them the status of universal laws and norms that in their own domain have a similar status to the laws of mathematics and the natural sciences.[10]

The conditions laid down by Habermas for achieving universal consent spell out very well an excellent ideal that may serve a heuristic and therapeutic purpose by giving us a goal to work for. Nevertheless, as with Frankena, it is as yet an unrealized hope that has such a utopian quality that we have no assurance that it will ever come to pass. It leaves unrefuted, even unscathed, the claim that the finitude, historicity, and cultural relativity of reason will prevent the ideal from ever becoming reality. More importantly, it neglects the fact of original sin, which here means the deep, stubborn, and ineradicable tendency of communities and individuals to pursue their own interests beyond what an impartial justice would permit and to use force in the securing of selfish ends. With Reinhold Niebuhr we may agree that no prior limits can be put on the extent to which egocentrism may be overcome.[11] Nevertheless, we have no empirical evidence from history to indicate that self-interest can be transcended in solidarity with others to permit the achievement of "ideal speech" conditions. The world is filled with inherited hatreds, suspicion and fear of "the Other," and the desire for power, glory, supremacy, and domination. The continuing controversies between the Israelis and the Palestinians indicate how historically-rooted hatreds and conflicts of interest impede progress toward reconciliation, peace, and tolerable compromises. If universal assent could be secured regarding justice, that would overcome the relativism that generates differences. The other problem, of course, is whether universal agreement is demonstration of rightness, if rightness means reflective of an objective moral order ingredient in the structure of reality. Nevertheless, if all agreed, that would certainly form the basis for a harmonious society, and that would in itself be a great gain.

Conclusion

To the extent that Rachels, Frankena, and Habermas are interested in that definition of rightness as conformity to reality, they would have to assume the union of reason and reality, i.e., the real is the rational, and the rational is the real. I do not doubt that the order of moral reality has a rational structure, but I think that love, the supreme virtue, has a transrational or ecstatic dimension that an ethic based purely on reason might miss. One could, I suppose, argue that reason can acknowledge this ecstatic dimension and thus its own limits. Nevertheless, human beings cannot know for sure that any of their schemes reproduce the patterns in the nature of things. If they believe that metaphysics can be bypassed or ignored, so that it is sufficient to talk about truths of reason without reference to reality, that raises a troubling question. What are the truths of reason about? To what do they refer? If there is no reference to patterns in the structure of reality, then what is their status? What makes them objectively valid? Truths of reason must state something that is true of something, or so it seems to me.

Isaiah Berlin spoke of three propositions that have been dominant in the mainstream of Western tradition: (1) All genuine questions have one answer that is true for everybody, everywhere, all the time. (2) A path leading to the discovery of these truths is in principle available to everyone. (3) All truths are compatible and form one harmonious whole.[12] In part, it depends on what 1 means. If it means there is no one perfect, conflict-free moral ideal absolutely valid for all societies, I agree. There may be equally excellent and equally reasonable but different ways of organizing the plurality of values in line with 3. There is one glory of Rome, another of Egypt and Greece. However, I am inclined to believe that there is an objective order or reality and morality that is what it is so that there can be only one true description of it. The problem is knowing when we are in possession of this one and only truth.

I have argued for two points: (a) universal agreement is no guarantee that the consensus conforms to objective reality, and (b) our only access to reality is through interpretations of experience that exhibit plurality and relativity. Hence, I agree wholeheartedly in rejecting 2 in that while in principle reality is accessible equally to all, in fact reason is rooted in particular historical perspectives and corrupted by self-interest, i.e., qualified by finitude and freedom.

With respect to 3 as far as ethics is concerned, I agree with Berlin in affirming a stubborn pluralism that insists that not all moral values can be realized simultaneously in individuals or societies without qualification, conflict, or limitation. Berlin insisted rightly that this in itself does not necessarily imply relativism but only a plurality of objectively valid perspectives not fully compatible with each other.

Rachels, Frankena, and Habermas seem to agree with 1 and 2 in ways I have contested. They may also accept 3, which is the most subtle and difficult. I agree that there are some moral imperatives that everybody ought to agree on whether they do or not. Torturing babies for the fun of it is absolutely wrong. Anybody who makes a rational case for the contrary contradicts the very idea of morality and moral constraint on behavior. Yet systems of ethics may assign different priorities to values in some cases that are equally rational and moral.

Values can be in tension with each other, and sometimes their claims may have equal weight, requiring a decision that reflects a subjective preference that is no less rational or moral than the opposite choice. Justice and mercy may sometimes be in such an equilibrium. Choosing to end one's life rather than to endure further suffering in some extreme cases may have equal rational and moral claim to objective validity with choosing to live on in spite of everything. Subjective preference that is relative to the suffering individual is the deciding factor that reason as such cannot question on universal, objective grounds.

Issues of social justice may present a similar problem. Freedom and equality can be complementary and mutually supportive, but they can also be in conflict. Capitalistic freedom may lead to great inequalities of income and wealth. Socialist equality may require coercion that restricts individual freedom. Can reason provide the one and only correct balancing and interrelationship between freedom and equality? I do not believe it can. Can three societies have different sets of preferences relating freedom and equality agreed to by large majorities that could claim to be equally rational and moral? I see no reason why not.

It would appear, then, that two types of relativities may emerge. They are sometimes difficult to distinguish but are worth noting. (1) The first has to do with subjective preferences that may be individual or social in a context in which many basic values are shared. In cases where an ensemble of interrelated values can be prioritized in different ways so that reason cannot render a clear verdict in favor of one weighting and balancing over the other, a decision has to be rendered by a community or individual reflecting subjective propensity. Here the basic values of the parties might be quite similar but differ in inclination because of a particular history or set of individual experiences that created a bias one way or the other. Subjective preference comes into play when reason offers no definitive resolution between two equally rational options. The "unforced force of the better reason" is ineffective, since the argument is about which reason is superior. I have suggested that the conflict between Nozick and Rawls on the priority to be given to equality cannot be absolutely settled by reason alone, although rational considerations play a major part. In the end, however, it is partly a matter of personal preference.[13]

(2) Deeper differences rooted in history and culture may produce more profound contrasts. It is one thing to compare twentieth century Sweden and the United States in which the former values equality more highly than the latter while sharing many democratic assumptions and values. It is another thing to compare either with a European monarchy of several centuries ago based on the divine right of kings in which freedom and equality for the masses have little standing. In 2 the differences are between two systems based on conflicting assumptions about what makes a government legitimate. How far can reason decide between absolute monarchy and modern constitutional democracy? A defense of the divine right of kings requires premises that simply have no standing in liberal democracies. Presumably, Rachels would argue that democracy is simply more reasonable. Given my assumptions, I agree. Frankena and Habermas would agree if that is the conclusion reached by an ideal rational community. I contend we have a splendid example

of the second kind of relativity and a paradigm of the basic kind of relativity I am defending. Rachels, Frankena, and Habermas think that, at least in the long run, reason can decide all these questions in a way that would command the assent of all unbiased, fully-informed, thoroughly competent rational agents. I maintain that resolution of moral problems is always dependent on the intellectual resources available, assumptions held regarding relevant fundamental matters, and the operative value preferences of communities and individuals.

I certainly agree that there appears to be a long-range tendency in history toward greater acceptance of ideas of democracy, individual freedom, and equality for all. (1) That could mean that global civilization is coming nearer to objective moral truth. From my subjective point of view that is the case. (2) It could also mean simply that global cultural consciousness is changing in a way that favors what we Americans believe. Practically speaking, it makes little difference as long as democracy prevails. My personal outlook inclines me to 1. My relativism and skepticism lead me to affirm 2 in factual terms. I hesitate, however, to conclude that this is identical with 1 with respect to the objective truth and universal validity of the normative values of democracy. That unresolved tension is probably the point at which my moral philosophy is most problematic.

Truths Of Revelation

A third way appeals to a higher source of moral knowledge than is available to human beings searching on their own. Many religious communities speak of a divine disclosure of truth that may or may not be accessible in whole or in part by reason alone. The many ways of relating reason and revelation in Christian thought are too extensive to be dealt with here. Suffice it to say that they range from almost total opposition to near unity with patterns of tension, conversion, and supplementation in between.[14] The standard claim is that in the history of Israel and in the person of Jesus of Nazareth is given by divine initiative a disclosure of religious and moral truth that is final, normative, and ultimate. The Bible is the authoritative witness to this unveiling of the deepest mysteries of life by the Creator of the world whose power and goodness are unsurpassable. For some the Word of God is contained in the words of the Bible, so that the right interpretation of them provides us with an infallible source of truth (Protestant fundamentalism). Others point to religious experience as the locus of divine self-disclosure and see the Bible as its expression in culturally-conditioned categories (Protestant liberalism). Some look to certain crucial events in the history of Israel as the bearer of a unique disclosure of God to which the Bible is the authoritative witness (Protestant neo-orthodoxy). Liberalism pointed to Jesus of Nazareth as the objective referent point of religious experience that yielded a normative disclosure of God. One strand of liberal thought focused on an internal or mystical apprehension of God that stressed feeling and awareness of divine presence (Schleiermacher). Another focused on Jesus as moral teacher, leader, example, and revealer of the character and purpose of God who by his ministry introduces believers into the Kingdom of God (Ritschl). Neo-orthodoxy saw in the Christ-event a normative revelation.

Liberal and neo-orthodox thought was able to make an accommodation to historical and cultural relativism by acknowledging a plurality of legitimate theological expressions while retaining an objective norm in the person, sayings, and mission of Jesus of Nazareth. The Bible was relativized while the Apostolic witness to Jesus as the Christ had priority over subsequent interpretations that were to be tested by it. The Christ-centered experience of God could be expressed in a variety of thought forms (liberalism). The Christ-event required a decision and a response of faith that could be interpreted in various concrete conceptual formulations and language systems (neo-orthodoxy). Liberalism spoke of experience and its expression; neo-orthodoxy talked about events and their interpretation. Both expression and interpretation were culturally-conditioned and historically relative. The Bible itself was not exempt from this relativity but nevertheless contained normative truth. The theological task was to find in them the essence or vital core or central meanings of biblical faith that defined Christian identity.

Two contemporary Protestant outlooks that accept pluralism and historical relativity continue the effort to come to terms with the modern mind while preserving Christian identity.[15] Post-liberal theology (Yale school) seeks a church theology that preserves historic Christian truth based on the Bible as a whole but makes no attempt to justify itself before the standards of present-day secular reason.[16] Revisionist theology (Chicago school) seeks a public theology that appeals to common human experience in the effort to correlate the gospel with the convincing elements of modern culture.[17] The distinction between the eternal truth of the gospel and the plurality of theological formulations that have arisen in history has produced numerous, irresolvable debates about the essence of Christianity that each version must contain in order to preserve Christian identity. Protestant modernists declared the search for a universal core of beliefs to be both hopeless and useless and insisted that present-day Christians were bound only to accept the highest and best of the tradition as judged by specific communities and individuals. This is the approach I have taken.[18]

The appeal to revelation at least acknowledges the historical particularity of truth claims. However, those within the Christian tradition usually claim that it provides universal truth. The appeal to revelation, however, provides no exemption from issues of universality and objective validity associated with natural law or the truths of reason. There is no way to prove that God is indeed the author of the claims said to be so authorized. Nor does the appeal to reason provide an escape from historical relativism and pluralism. All systems of philosophy are as historically particular as the Christian tradition. In this sense, reason and revelation are on the same footing and have the same problems though coming at them from different directions.

I have maintained, to use a theological term, that all truth claims in morality and religion are matters of faith. We see what we see because we stand where we stand. Faith in epistemological terms means historic perspective. We all walk by faith and not by sight. Morality and religion are matters of belief, not of certain knowledge. Truth is received as a gift that evokes a response of accepting faith. A parallel can be found in philosophical inquiry to experiencing a disclosure, a sense of being grasped by what commands assent that one can only accept as a gift.[19] For Christians, faith in

Christ provides the clue, the orienting insight, the starting point. Epistemologically, this simply means having a particular historical location with antecedents. Philosophers are in the same position. Their point of orientation is also a historical location with antecedents. They are utilitarians or Kantians, Platonists or Aristotelians, realists or pragmatists, and so on. They belong to identifiable schools of thought rooted in history.

This does not mean that all talk about revelation should be abandoned. It means only that we need to seek an understanding of what it means that makes it a legitimate partner in moral discourse. More than half a century ago H. Richard Niebuhr gave us the starting point theology needs today.

> *Theology, then, must begin in history and with Christian history because it has no choice; in this sense it is forced to begin with revelation, meaning by that word historic faith.... Such a theology of revelation is objectively relativistic, proceeding with confidence in the independent reality of what is seen though recognizing that its assertions about that reality are meaningful only to those who look upon it from the same standpoint.*[20]

To say that Christian ethics is based on divine revelation, then, means simply that it makes its inquiries into right and wrong from within the Christian tradition. It asks what rights, duties, and virtues are characteristic of that perspective. This involves critical investigation, analysis, and assessment to clear away what is incidental or aberrant in order to locate what is central and deep in it as dis-closed by an examination of the Scriptures. If this takes the form of a search for the essence of Christianity, two qualifications are necessary. (1) It is not self-evident or certain that a self-defining core is objectively present within the diversity of the New Testament in any categorical sense waiting to be discovered. (2) All such inquiries produce only what the interpreter thinks to be essential. It is better to make a simple confession that says, "This is what I find to be most important in the tradition, and I think it is basic and not peripheral to its total witness." A debate about what is the heart of the matter is a waste of time and never produces any useful results as far as I can tell. It is more fruitful to deal with the content of operational theologies and ethical standards that command the loyalty of enough people to make them important.

Particular communities, of course, at some point find it necessary to define the boundaries of their own faith in order to have enough unity and integrity for them to function effectively. This, however, is a practical matter of defining the beliefs and practices that constitute a particular group, consent to which is a prerequisite of membership. It is a matter of self-definition for operational purposes. It need not be done on absolutist, dogmatic grounds that claim exclusive validity for its version of the gospel. It need not involve the claim that *our gospel* is *the gospel* but only a clarification of the rules of participation necessary to the existence of a community. Communities have every right to be as narrow or as inclusive, as restrictive or as permissive, as they choose to be. Where the lines of exclusion are drawn is up to each particular community. It is not easy to maintain a healthy balance between unity and diversity. An unavoidable tension exists between intensity of commitment with insistence on unity and broad inclusiveness that permits a wide range of differences. Communities simply have to define themselves in this regard, since no objective ideal free from the ambiguity of pluses and minuses can be specified *a priori*.

One additional problem for the appeal to revelation is that the revelation must be interpreted. Whether the medium of revelation is the Bible, experience, certain events, or something else, someone has to spell out the content of what is given by special divine disclosure and say what it means in contemporary language for problems people face here and now. I contend that in the final analysis the interpreter is the functional authority, whatever objective basis may be claimed. Consider the following:

The Word of God
The Will of God
The Bible
The Christ-event
What Jesus teaches, shows by example, would do, have us do
Religious experience
Whatever is claimed to be the source of divine revelation

All of these translate practically into what I or somebody (the church, a council, community decision, or whatever) decides is the correct interpretation of revelation located in the Word of God, the Bible, the example, teachings of Jesus, and so on throughout the whole list. It is interpretation that finally counts. That is what we concretely deal with. The Bible says a lot of things but means very little until someone interprets its varied and diverse witness in contemporary terms. Consider how Christians have wrestled with the "hard sayings" in the Sermon on the Mount (Matthew 5:27-38) and drawn conflicting conclusions.

However, what is said about the appeal to revelation applies equally to the appeal to reason. It is finally what I or somebody thinks reason requires me to believe that counts. Consider the following:

What can be justified
Objective, universal truth
The right thing to do
What will achieve the greatest good
Natural law
What has the best reasons in support of it
What an ideal rational community will ultimately assent to
Whatever else might be added to this inventory to complete it

Operationally, all of the above come down to mean what some interpreter believes to be _____ (fill in the blank with any of the above).

What communities and individuals believe about morality and what they can persuade others to agree to is functionally what we deal with in practice. History is filled with a plurality of belief systems and moral codes. We could add dreams, visions, readings of chicken entrails, deliverances from aliens from outer space, messages found under rocks, and so on through a long list. Whatever the authorities people appeal to, they believe what they believe. They justify their convictions by criteria that are internal to their belief systems, i.e., that constitute part of the belief system itself. While living in obedience to what they cannot deny, communities and individuals interact in various ways ranging from conflict and mutual condemnation to passive coexistence and toleration. Ideally, they will engage in peaceful conversation with each other in mutual respect and be open to change when so persuaded. No one has so far and is not likely to find a way to reduce the plurality of belief by some final discovery that commands the assent of all so that everything else is tossed onto the trash pile of error. To put it differently, there is no supertheory that can resolve disputes between mere theories. All we have are the contending theories themselves. All attempted resolutions and efforts finally to get it right are just other theories. Hence, a pragmatism is called for that finds ways of accommodation that work situationally. We can make alliances for political purposes on particular issues while continuing to disagree on others. We can contend with opponents and fight for what we believe with every means proportionate to the seriousness of the issue — including the use of force as a last resort if great evil can be prevented or great and justifying ends can be achieved no other way. All of this involves a good deal of muddling through, compromising here, standing firm there. We can try to combine confidence in our own insights with humility that recognizes our own limitations, biases, self-interest, and other impediments that are likely to cloud our vision. We can and must act as if we had the truth while recognizing the historicity, contingency, and relativity of our point of view and all points of view.

The human predicament is that operationally agreement is the best we can hope for in confirmation of our own beliefs. We cannot examine reality to see if our theories about it are correct. All such investigations proceed from some particular perspective with built in criteria that reflect some theory of reality already held. They produce not a comparison of theory with reality but only one more theory about reality. We cannot examine uninterpreted reality in order to test our interpretations of it except by making use of an interpretation of reality to do so. When we do, what we get is another interpretation that remains as uncertain and as relative to history, culture, and individual outlook as all the others. We can examine interpreted reality as experienced and seek for a better interpretation that more satisfactorily accounts for evidence and is more coherent with all our other beliefs. In practice, then, what we have is a plurality of interpretations that must come to terms with each other in some fashion. Debates about which interpretation is the true one are useless, hopeless, and a waste of time.

The conclusion of the matter is that there is no way of acquiring moral truth that is *the way*. There are only multiple ways that various communities employ. This is the fact, stubborn, irreducible, persistent, and ineradicable, that we must come to terms with in practical terms. By trying to stand where others stand, we may see some of what they see, and if others make an effort to look at things from our vantage point, they may discover what we are convinced of. Altogether we may grow in mutual appreciation and find widening circles of agreement while we continue to do what we must and believing what we cannot deny. We can do so maintaining our own integrity while not despising the insights of others. We can oppose them when we cannot do otherwise without betraying our own loves, loyalties, convictions, and commitments. But there is a givenness about the plurality of communities of belief and practice that cannot be avoided but can only be dealt with pragmatically and situationally doing the best we can. In the end we can do no more than join with Martin Luther in honest confession: "Here I stand; I can do no other."

In the chapter following I will begin to set forth my views on the theory and practice of Christian ethics.

Endnotes

1. For a defense and some contemporary versions of natural law theory, see Robert P. George, *In Defense of Natural Law* (Oxford: Oxford University Press, 1999), and Robert P. George, ed., *Natural Law Theory: Contemporary Essays* (Oxford: Clarendon Press, 1992). For recent religious perspectives on natural law, see Michael Cromartie, ed., *A Preserving Grace: Protestants, Catholics, and Natural Law* (Grand Rapids: Eerdman's Publishing Co., 1997).

2. I have argued for this principle in *Process Ethics: A Constructive System* (Lewiston, NY: Edwin Mellen Press, 1984), 195-310.

3. David Tracy proposes that correspondence be interpreted to mean "the consensual truth of warranted beliefs" and that correspondence models of truth

be retained as important but not primary. David Tracy, *Plurality and Ambiguity: Hermeneutics, Religion, Hope* (San Francisco: Harper & Row, 1987), 29. This view stands in the tradition of John Dewey, who spoke of "warranted assertibility."

4. The three points are a direct quote from James Rachels, *Elements of Moral Philosopyr*, 2nd ed. (New York: McGraw-Hill, 1993), 40.

5. Here I am conflating two issues: disagreements over what is *objectively* valid as determined by reason and value preferences that are *subjectively* derived. I will say more about this later in the chapter. I do insist that both are involved in the total picture of relativity.

6. Reinhold Niebuhr, *An Interpretation of Christian Ethics* (New York: Charles Scribner's Sons, 1935), *The Nature and Destiny of Man* (New York: Charles Scribner's Sons, 1949), II, 68-97, 244-86.

7. See my *Science, Secularization, and God* (Nashville: Abingdon Press, 1969), 191-2. To put it another way, God freely and spontaneously chooses and wills what love requires. Love is not a standard outside of and independent of God but a description of God's own nature, since God is love. Cf. Paul Tillich, *Systematic Theology* (Chicago: University of Chicago Press, 1951), I, 174-86, 247-8.

8. William K. Frankena, *Ethics*, 2nd ed. (Englewood Cliffs: Prentice-Hall, 1973), 112.

9. *Ibid.*

10. Jürgen Habermas, *Toward a Rational Society* (Boston: Beacon Press, 1971), *Justification and Application: Remarks on Discourse Ethics* (Cambridge: Polity Press, 1983), *The Theory of Communicative Action, Volume One: Reason and the Rationalization of Society* (Boston: Beacon Press, 1984), *The Theory of Communicative Action, Volume Two: The Critique of Functionalist Reason* (Boston: Beacon Press, 1987), and *Moral Consciousness and Communicative Action* (Cambridge, MA: The MIT Press, 1990).

11. Reinhold Niebuhr, *The Nature and Destiny of Man*, I, 150-300. See also, *Faith and History* (New York: Charles Scribner's Sons, 1949).

12. See Michael Ignatieff, *Isaiah Berlin: A Life* (New York: Metropolitan Books, 1998).

13. In *The Passion for Equality* (Totowa, NJ: Rowman & Littlefield, 1987), 131-42, I argued that Nozick was wrong in assuming that economic production could be reduced to individual transactions, contending that it is a social process. Is Frankena's distinction between basic and derivative values useful here? If Nozick acknowledged my point, would that make a difference? Do Nozick and I disagree on factual matters but share the same basic values? I doubt it. Agreement on factual matters is important in this case, but I suspect that it is not the crucial point. It is more probable that the greater priority given to equality by Rawls and me comes down to a matter of personal value preference, although it is a difficult point. Can reason decide the priority to be given to freedom and equality and under what circumstances? I doubt it beyond a certain point.

14. A splendid treatment detailing five patterns of relating reason and revelation can be found in H. Richard Niebuhr, *Christ and Culture* (New York: Harper & Brothers, 1951).

15. For a good discussion and critique of both viewpoints, see William Placher, *Unapologetic Theology: A Christian Voice in a Pluralistic Conversation* (Louisville: Westminster/John Knox, 1989).

16. See George A. Lindbeck, *The Nature of Doctrine* (Philadelphia: Westminster Press, 1984).

17. See David Tracy, *Blessed Rage for Order: The New Pluralism in Theology* (New York: The Seabury Press, 1975).

18. See my *The Impact of American Religious Liberalism* (New York: Harper & Row, 1962), for a detailed description of liberal and neo-orthodox modes of thought. For my version of modernism, see my *Theological Biology: The Case for a New Modernism* (Lewiston, NY: Edwin Mellen Press, 1991), and *Toward New Modernism* (Lanham, MD: University Press of America, 1997).

19. Cf. Paul Tillich, *Systematic Theology*, I, 9. Tillich maintains that all ontologies originate in a *mystical a priori*, an experience of something ultimate that is grasped intuitively. If in the course of investigation this ultimate is discovered, it is because it was there from the beginning. All spiritual reasoning is circular in this fashion.

20. H. Richard Niebuhr, *The Meaning of Revelation* (New York: The Macmillan Co., 1946), 21-2. This is an intriguing passage. Niebuhr speaks of "confidence in the independent reality of what is seen." I am more of a skeptic who cannot be so sure. I do agree with him in recognizing that the assertions of faith "about that reality are meaningful only to those who look upon it from the same standpoint."

Chapter 5
The Ethics Of Christian Belief: Theory

Two parts of the ethics of belief are especially relevant here. (1) Ethicists by using the resources of ethics as a formal discipline cannot tell us what is right and wrong. They can only tell us what they believe to be right or wrong. (2) The proper place for ethicists to begin is with the theories and practices of some community or of its members in order to describe, analyze, assess, and revise these moral beliefs as seems appropriate.

I propose to follow each of these premises. (1) I offer my beliefs, my interpretation of the moral life and what it requires of us in order to avoid what is wrong and do what is right. (2) I begin with the moral tradition of the Christian community, specifically as grounded in the New Testament. Since Christians are divided into a wide variety of sub-communities on a global scale, the problem of choice is complicated. Any decision as to how to pare this down will be quite arbitrary. I have chosen to speak broadly of the biblical outlook rather than of the history of a particular communion. This focus on the Bible will clearly identify me as a Protestant, and my pronounced — excessive? — individualism is fitting for my Baptist identity. This further entangles the matter and requires additional decisions as to how to proceed. One might begin with the Baptist and closely-related communities that emerged in the sixteenth and seventeenth centuries. The ethical themes characteristic of the early congregations could be outlined. Ethics was of central importance to the radical sects of the Reformation. Merit attaches to beginning with their emphasis on living a holy life. Yet Baptists in the year 2000 are so much a part of the mainstream of American religious life that they are hardly an ethically distinct group any more. My friend Will Campbell once said that Baptists were the hope of the world today — if only we could find some! Theologically, economically, socially, and morally, Baptist congregations and members are all over the place. Unfortunately, zip codes are in many cases a better indication of the moral outlook of Baptists and other Christians than their denominational affiliation.[1] Too many theological and social factors have adulterated the early sectarian tendencies to make early Baptist traditions a useful starting point.[2] A certain messiness and individuality attaches to being a contemporary Baptist that exceeds what would be the case for more hierarchical, authoritarian, and tradition-bound communions. Hence, I propose in arbitrary fashion to carry on the conversation with the biblical perspective from the standpoint of a twentieth century Christian believer. In so doing my Protestant background and Baptist individualism will shine through. It matters that I am a trained theologian with a bias for the poor and oppressed who has forty years of teaching experience. It is important that I grew up in rural Georgia in the 1930s and '40s among farmers and mill workers. It is significant that I am a liberal in theology, politics, and social philosophy. What follows is a perspective on biblical and Christian ethics from that vantage point, acknowledged to be thoroughly relative, time- and culture-bound, and dependent on my individual background, including my education in a liberal Protestant seminary. I would only add that all other interpreters approach the Christian tradition and current moral issues from a standpoint that is equally conditioned by history, culture, denominational background, and individual peculiarities. All interpretations can be contested by others and tested by everyone with good effect by comparing them with the biblical texts, though every tester will also view the objective materials from a conditioned subjective standpoint.

An Interpretation Of Christian Ethics

Christian ethics is based on the religious traditions of ancient Israel and the witness of the New Testament to the revelation of God in Jesus regarded as the expected Christ. Human morality is seen in the context of God's action in creation and in the history of Israel, especially in the incarnation of God in Jesus and his saving work through his death and resurrection. Salvation in the New Testament focuses on spiritual deliverance from the power and guilt of sin, emancipation from demonic powers, and the hope of inheriting the Kingdom (Society)[3] of God that was expected in its fullness soon. Nevertheless, it includes the fulfillment of the bodily and social aspects of existence as well. We are expected to feed the hungry, heal the sick, and assist the poor. This emphasis follows from the conviction that the material creation is good and that bodily life in history is meaningful. The hope for the resurrection of the body at the Endtime is eloquent witness to this. It implies the reality and worth of individual selfhood, and the goodness of life in its physical dimensions, and the value of historical and temporal events. While a right relationship to God is central to both Testaments, the Hebrew Bible comparatively focuses more on the fulfillment of human existence in its historical and social setting. The Hebrew prophets focused on peace, righteousness, and prosperity as the hallmarks of the coming New Age. It involved a wholeness, fullness, and enjoyment of life in a setting of justice and harmony of all with all, including animals as well as human beings (Isaiah 9:1-7, 11:1-9; Micah 4:1-5). The overcoming of sin and its power to degrade and destroy life is central to the purpose of perfecting the world but is by no means the whole of it. The good life is joyful existence centering in the praise of God and the love of all God's creatures in a harmonious setting in which all suffering has been banished and all that is destructive of justice and happiness is no more. Morality has to do with human responsibility in promoting peace, justice, universal concord, and mutual love as the appropriate response to God's activity in creating finite beings and directing them toward complete fulfillment in a life of blessedness and pure delight.

The virtuous life is depicted in the Bible in a number of ways. We are to live in obedience to the will of God, who as Creator, Sovereign Lord, and Savior has every right to require us to obey (Exodus 20:1-2). We are to do justice, love mercy, and walk humbly with our God (Amos 5, Micah 6:8). We are to seek the mind of Christ and follow his example (Philippians 2:1-11). We are to live in freedom empowered by the Spirit whose fruits are love, peace, and joy (Romans 8, Galatians 5). We are to live in accordance with the righteousness of the Kingdom (Matthew 5-7). We are to love God with all our hearts and our neighbors as we love ourselves (Luke 10:25-28, Romans 12:8-10, 1 Corinthians 13). A number of specific requirements are laid out in the pages of both Testaments (Exodus 20:3-17, Romans 12-15, Ephesians 5-6, Colossians 3-4) in these and in too many other passages throughout to be mentioned. Paul urges that love is the fulfilling of the law — all of it (Romans 13:8-10). All of these are part of the picture, but the question arises as to whether there is a useful way of organizing and simplifying the large body of diverse materials dealing with the moral life developed over more than a thousand years.

Commentators over the generations have offered a large assortment of ways to order the many ethical themes of Scripture in accordance with some overall scheme. Only within such an interpretive framework can we give unity, systematic coherence, comprehensiveness, and simplicity to the variety of texts that make up the Scriptural witness. Examination of this history is beyond the scope of this endeavor.[4] Many of them are useful and have merit in finding the big themes in all the many parts of the Bible. None of them can convincingly be called the right or correct one demanded by the Bible itself. All of them are constructions with varying degrees of merit with accompanying limitations. I offer one way of putting it all together in an inclusive manner that is both illuminating without excessive distortion of the many texts that have to be considered. Yet, like all the others, mine imposes a pattern of unity on a stubborn multiplicity for which no exclusive or final claim can be made. I offer it as a contribution to an ongoing and never conclusive discussion.[5]

In *The Ethics of Enjoyment* I claimed that in the biblical witness the will of God is to make heaven real.[6] The aim of God is to create and perfect a people and a cosmos. God is at work in the world creating a royal and loyal people and directing them toward a good future. In the coming Society the joy of life will be complete in a perfected community. Joined by bonds of love to each other and having their unity in the praise of God, the heavenly inhabitants enjoy the supreme bliss of a completely fulfilled life. The theme of a good future takes many forms throughout the Bible. In the beginning Abraham is promised that his descendants will have many children and that they will bless the world (Genesis 12:1-3). In the end John (Revelation 21) is given a magnificent vision of the New Jerusalem coming down out of heaven in all its radiant splendor. In between are varying conceptions of the good future that God has promised. But throughout them all runs the idea that the will of God is to make heaven real.

Moral action is the fitting response of human beings to the work of God in the world to make heaven real by which life is created and directed toward fulfillment. In his study of New Testament ethics, C.H. Dodd claims that the moral imperative can be stated like this: Reproduce in your actions toward others the quality and the direction of the saving acts of God toward you.[7] The quality of God's action is love. Hence, we should love each other as God has loved us. The love (*agape*) of God toward us becomes the norm of the *agape* that we show toward others. The direction or aim of God's action is the actualization of the Society of God on earth. In the New Testament the Society comes as a gift of God to those who prepare for its coming by living in accordance with its requirements. Repentance, faith, hope, and love are the marks of those who will enter the Society (Mark 1:14-5, Luke 10:25-7). To reproduce the aim and direction of God's actions is to make the actualization of the Society our supreme goal.[8] We do so by promoting the fulfillment of the potential for enjoyment of all persons in community. Trusting God, loving others, and promoting their good is the appropriate response to the gift and demand of the gospel that proclaims the coming of the Society of God. The moral imperative, then, can be put in two sets of language, which coincide in meaning. Stated philosophically the principle is this: Respond to the creation of life in the evolutionary process by honoring the intrinsic value of living beings and by promoting the fulfillment of their potential. Stated theologically, the principle is this: Respond to the action of God in creation and redemption by loving others as God has loved you and by cooperating with God in the actualizing of the Society of God on earth.

Moral action takes place in a concrete context in which we act as beings who are acted upon by other beings. Hence, inevitably and factually we do the right and seek the good as a response to what is happening in light of our interpretation of how we are constituted and shaped by what is going on in the world.[9] The statement that we are to reproduce in our actions the quality and aim of God's prior action on us sounds like a deontological imperative. It is better understood, I think, as an acknowledgment and description of the fact that moral action takes place in a system of activities which create and mold us and which require some interpretation of the total social and ontological situation in which moral action occurs. Moral action *is* a response. How we respond depends on how we understand the bases of obligation (deontological) and aspiration (teleological) within the factual framework within which we live and act.[10] This means that, in one sense, all ethics is contextual ethics. A complete ethical theory will interpret the context of moral action, that is, its ultimate ontological setting which determines what the right and the good are. The more precise statement of the moral imperative I have derived from C.H. Dodd, then, would read as follows: When you respond to what is happening to you, the fitting way of response is to do the right (love your neighbor) and seek the good (the Society of God) by reproducing the pattern of God's action toward you. In so doing you will be aligning yourself with reality, for the truth of the gospel is that God loves us and our neighbors and seeks the good of us all.

Christian love, of course, finds its source, its inspiration, and the definition of its nature in the New Testament interpretation of Jesus (Romans 5:8). The life of service which led to a sacrificial death is the measure of the heights to which *agape* rises. "Greater love has no man than this, that he lay down his life for his friends" (John 15:13 RSV). The prodigality of this love poured out for sinners, for enemies, for the neighbor in need is boundless. It is rooted in grace and comes spontaneously and unmotivated to us from God to become the pattern and norm of our responsibility toward others. *Agape* in the New Testament is grounded in a religious vision of a gracious, merciful God whose love for us is unconditional, extravagant, marvelous, and mysterious. It evokes faith and an answering love in us which accepts the gracious forgiveness offered us. The gratitude felt in the believer for this unmerited favor expresses itself in spontaneous and joyful service of the neighbor modeled after the self-giving which led Jesus to the cross. In this sense, while New Testament ethics can be understood as a prescription of what we ought to, this outlook can better be thought of as a description of what we will actually do in response to the grace of God so freely given to us. In gratitude for the love of God toward us, we will love God and neighbor as a spontaneous expression of who we are. We love because we have first been loved. What we will do is what we ought to do. We cannot love by deciding to do so. We love as an expression of our moral character. If we are to love each other, we must become loving persons. We become loving persons by first being loved. We love God because God first loved us (1 John 4:19). We love others even when they do not deserved to be loved because we were loved when we did not deserve to be loved (Romans 5:8). Hence, while appearing as a commandment, the imperative to love neighbor is better understood as a description of the fact that having been first loved, we will respond in gratitude in a spontaneous outpouring of love toward deserving and undeserving neighbors.[11]

The boundlessness of *agape*, its heedlessness of self, its prodigality in pouring itself out for the neighbor without counting the costs is undeniable as we read its character on the pages of the New Testament. The question is how we should understand the ethics of *agape* in the twenty-first century. In particular, does the sacrificial self-giving which is so prominent in the New Testament rule out a legitimate love of self in a defense of its just interests, and a quest for its own fulfillment? The New Testament does not explicitly settle this issue on textual grounds. No systematic definition of terms appears. The questions we raise in the midst of complexities, ambiguities, compromises, conflicting obligations, and unavoidable trade-offs simply were not addressed by the New Testament writers.

Generated in the hot fervor of apocalyptic expectations and motivated by an appeal to religious absolutes, the New Testament states an unconditional ethical ideal without regard to it practicality in a continuing society for which one takes responsibility. But we must deal with its practical application. When we translate the ethics of Jesus and of the New Testament into a workable guide for living in a contemporary society, a congruence arises with the morality I have developed in the form of a Christian natural ethics that I developed in my *Process Ethics*.[12] There I maintained that the ethical imperative could be stated in a double form: honor the intrinsic value of living beings, especially persons (deontological version), and promote their enjoyment or happiness or fulfillment (teleological version).[13] Much more clearly than I understood then, I would now want to insist that these imperatives are also descriptives. As imperatives, they elucidate the standard by which the moral life is measured — the ethical norm. As descriptives, they are statements of how we will act when our character reaches full maturity, having been formed in intimate communities in which we were loved and learned to love others as God and those nearest to us have first loved us.

Christian love is *agape*. A correspondence, if not identity, obtains between *agape* and the philosophical claim that we are obligated to honor the intrinsic worth of every person. *Agape* is regard for the neighbor as a person independent of the special qualities or moral merit of a given individual.[14] *Agape* is identification with the interests of the neighbor in disregard of the other person's attractiveness. The Christian moral imperative requires the believer to meet the needs and promote the welfare of persons as persons. Hence, every individual human being is equal to every other. *Agape* is active concern for the other which is permanent and unalterable. Nothing the neighbor can do, be, or become can erase the fundamental obligation on the part of the believer to be attentive to the needs and welfare of the other as a person. *Agape* is unconditional active concern for other human beings. It does not ask whether the other is deserving or whether the love shown is returned or acknowledged in any way. It is not withheld even from the enemy or from those who hate the lover. In all these ways I see an identity between *agape* and the moral norm I have proposed on philosophical grounds. Every person has intrinsic worth, and we are obligated to honor that worth. This is another way of saying that one should have equal regard for all persons as persons. Christian love is, of course, set within the context of the Christian vision of reality and the proclamation of the gospel. However, there is a coincidence of normative content between *agape* and the philosophical imperative to reverence the intrinsic worth of persons.

Likewise, I believe there is a congruence between the New Testament norm of promoting the Society of God and actualizing the human potential for enjoyment. The idea of the good future that God will bring into being suggests an ideal society in which all the needs of the body and of the spirit are met. It implies a complete triumph of good over evil. It is a community in which the wholeness and fullness of life are completely actualized so that joy reigns supreme. The idea of the coming End in which the people of God will inherit the destiny God intends for them undergoes a long period of development and takes a variety of forms. Not all of these can be reconciled with each other. In the New Testament the hope for the coming Society is set within an apocalyptic context in which the New Age is to be brought into being by a direct and sudden divine intervention. The Society of God is to be instituted by a cosmic miracle in which all sin and evil are conquered absolutely and forever.

The New Testament picture of the end of history cannot be taken literally, for things did not actually work out that way. History still continues. When the New Testament idea of the Society is translated into contemporary language that is both credible and relevant, it is congruent with the ethical imperative to maximize the enjoyment that accompanies the fulfillment of human potential. The Society comes insofar as the potential for enjoyment is actualized in individuals living in community with others. Just as with the New Testament idea of *agape*, the conception of the Society of God is set within a framework of theological assumptions and claims. But the ethical implications of a contemporary reconstruction of that ideal society coincide with the philosophically based norm of enjoyment as the supreme good of life.

Likewise, in both cases there is close connection between the biblical affirmation of a Creator and Redeemer whose will is to make heaven real and the philosophical assertion of a creativity in nature which has elaborated an increasingly complex hierarchy of life forms. These life forms are driven and drawn toward the enjoyment-producing fulfillment of their potential. Moreover, these experiencing subjects have intrinsic value which moral beings are obligated to respect. Whether seen biblically or philosophically, human life arises in a context of value-producing activities rooted in the depths of reality. We are acted upon by other beings and by the Ultimate Source of our being and of all beings. In that framework we have to respond to what is going on around us in the light of some interpretation of the meaning and direction of the cosmic process which gave us birth and being. Biblically and philosophically my claim is that we live in a goal-directed system of activities in which experiencing subjects find satisfaction by mutually-supportive relationships with persons and other living forms in the universal quest for fulfillment. Hence, a convergence of claims at the ethical level appears between the philosophical and biblical sources of the vision being set forth here. It holds also at the cosmic level of interpretation. God the Creator and Redeemer seeking to make heaven real — a creative cosmos evolving ever higher forms of enjoyment seeking living beings: these are alternative ways of approaching one central truth about reality and morality.

Stating the moral imperative in contemporary terms must account for the New Testament idea that the Society comes primarily as a gift. Jesus and the early church expected the end of the Old Age to come soon and suddenly by direct action of God. The Society is an objective reality that is coming. The idea is not that if people repent of their sins and love their neighbors, the Society will come. Rather the message is that the Society is coming, therefore the only appropriate thing to do is repent and live righteously.

Nevertheless, the Society has already begun to come in the ministry of Jesus. It is present wherever the power of God is at work casting out demons, healing the sick, forgiving sins, and making life whole. The response of the believer in loving actions is a public and visible manifestation of the presence of the Society. By reproducing the quality and direction of God's action, the community of the faithful become co-creators of the Society. A problem is posed by the fact that we live, as they did not, in the expectation that history will continue indefinitely without being ended suddenly by a cosmic transformation. How can this apocalyptic version of the Society which proved to be untrue in any literal sense be reinterpreted for persons living in 2000 and beyond?

We awaken into consciousness in a world that is prior to us and which we did not create. Life comes to us as a gift in all its complexity and with all its marvelous potential for enjoyment. Over billions of years an incredible, marvelous adventure has taken place. Some creativity at the base of things has brought life into being out of simple matter-energy and perhaps ultimately from nothing or pure possibility. Human beings have emerged from a long process. We inherit the gift of life with its persistent drive toward fulfillment in all of its myriad forms. We can plant and we can water but only God gives the increase of growth that leads to the harvest. It happens by itself when we cultivate. We can engage in sexual intercourse, but the production of new life in the most fundamental sense is not our act. The processes by which a fertilized egg becomes a healthy baby at birth occur by themselves. They happen apart from our will. So it is with all the satisfactions and pleasures we experience. The potentiality that is actualized by our cooperative action is a given and the enjoyment we experience is a gift. Moreover, there is a drive in the cosmic process toward the production and fulfillment of ever higher forms of life. Evolution is future-oriented and goal-directed. It pushes toward the perfection of its possibilities by creating more complex living beings with greater ranges and depths of experience and enjoyment.

The biblical theme of the Society of God points to the intention of God to create a people and to bring that community into a perfected future. The most productive framework for a contemporary reinterpretation of this motif is the theory of emergent evolution. A creative purpose at work in the cosmos has produced an ascending order of life forms of increasing complexity culminating on earth with the appearance of human beings. The promise of the Society's coming in all its fullness has not yet been realized and the ultimate future of the evolutionary adventure on earth is hidden in mystery. Yet in both perspectives human beings live a life of response to the givenness of creation and the potential of the future. They can enter creatively into the unfolding of the human quest for justice and joy, but they do so in cooperation with realities and possibilities that confront them as a gift with promise. The fitting response to the action of God upon us in the evolutionary process is to love our neighbors by honoring their intrinsic value as persons and to promote the coming of the Society by actualizing the potential for enjoyment in community.

Love-fulfilling and Society-of-God-promoting actions are interdependent and complementary. They require and presuppose each other. Love of neighbor expresses the reality of the Society. Society-promoting actions manifest a love of neighbor. Deontological obligation incarnate in loving service of the neighbor is joined to teleological aspiration embodied in Society-seeking strategies. If not pressed too far, a distinction in orientation may be useful in seeing the relationship between love and the Society. Love begins with a focus on the nearest neighbor here and now. It directs attention to immediate needs. It compels us to attack the worst evils of the moment. However, in order to meet the needs of our neighbors and to relieve human misery here and now, it is necessary for ethical action to take account of present social structures and future possibilities. The social order must be transformed in accordance with the imperatives of justice. In this way love moves toward the concerns growing out of the quest of the Society. Promoting the Society of God on earth directs attention to the social order and to its ideal possibilities. It has a future orientation which takes the whole of society into account. Society of God ethics obligates us to create the kind of social order that is most likely to increase human welfare and promote the enjoyment of all. From that vantage point, it proceeds toward meeting the needs and enhancing the welfare of individuals in the present. Hence, each orientation moves toward and merges with the other.

In connection with the interdependence and complementarity of love-fulfilling and Society-of-God-promoting actions, love should not be interpreted strictly in either deontological or teleological terms. Both points of view are plausible. The law of love should be taken in the most comprehensive sense to mean that one should honor the intrinsic worth and promote the welfare of the neighbor. Likewise, the imperative to actualize the Society obligates one to meet the neighbor's need here and now. The Society is manifest where the hungry are fed and the sick are healed at the moment. In this way a deontological element is added to the teleological quest for future actualization of Society possibilities in the more universal and long range sense. Hence, if love is given some deontological primacy, that does not mean that a teleological element is not present.

Agape: Sacrificial Or Mutual Love?

Prominent among the issues pertaining to the meaning of *agape* is the relation of self-love to neighbor-love. Jesus approved of the idea that we should love our neighbor as we love ourselves (Luke 10:25-28). But what does that mean? Does *agape* include the self among those to be taken into account, or does it require a sacrifice of the self for the sake of the neighbor? Three positions have been taken in recent years. (1) The first negates self-love and requires a purely sacrificial view of *agape* (Reinhold Niebuhr, Anders Nygren).[15] We should love our neighbors in the ethical sense in the same way that by nature we love ourselves, but that means caring for the neighbor instead of the self. (2) The second regards self-love as a derivative of neighbor-love. I can have regard for myself to the extent that it is necessary as a perquisite for serving others (Paul Ramsey).[16] (3) The third regards self and neighbor as worthy of equal treatment. *Agape* is then interpreted as mutual love (Daniel Day Williams).[17] Sacrifice of the self is required only when the neighbor's need exceeds my own or when the greater good of the community as a whole necessitates it.

I propose to defend the view that *agape* is best understood as equalitarian or mutual love and to do so in engagement with Reinhold Niebuhr, than whom there is still no greater exponent of Christian ethics more than a half-century later. The highest form of rational ethics according to Reinhold Niebuhr is mutual love — a giving and receiving in which all parties are considered equal in value.[18] While there is much to commend this ideal, he believes that it is unstable and will tend to degenerate into a calculation of benefits and ultimately disintegrate. Each party will anxiously be concerned about whether as much love is being returned as is being offered. Niebuhr is correct, I think, if one assumes that mutual love is conditional upon an equality of contribution and reward. Conditional mutual love says, "I will love you as much as you love me but only as long as I am getting as much as I give."

Niebuhr argues that mutual love must be constantly replenished by sacrificial love that is rooted in a faith in a transcendent God and thus not bound to this world's goods and standards only. Niebuhr thinks that sacrificial love is the core meaning of *agape* in the New Testament. *Agape* so understood stands as a transcendent standard beyond all human achievement, an "impossible possibility" that is yet relevant to every moral situation as judge, guide, and inspiration. This form of love is modeled after the example of Jesus on the cross. It sacrifices self in order to serve the other. It risks all and gives all, heedless of the self's own needs, wants, and interests. This love goes the second mile, resists not one who is evil, gives to everyone who would borrow, returns good for evil, and so on (Matthew 5:38-48).

I find this unqualified imperative to be morally inadequate in that it neglects necessary discriminations among persons and circumstances, puts no limits on obligation, and has no place for merit. If taken as an actual norm to be lived out, it indiscriminately and indeterminately requires the weak to sacrifice for the strong, the sick to sacrifice for the healthy, the poor to sacrifice for the rich, the virtuous to sacrifice for scoundrels, and the oppressed to sacrifice for the oppressor. Without some guard against this implication, justice is violated, and the worth, integrity, and dignity of the self are compromised. This way of putting it may be unfair to

Niebuhr in not sufficiently representing his full outlook. First of all, he does include mutuality, reciprocity, and equality as valid considerations. Sometimes reciprocity does occur, and in this fact is to be found the moral component in history. Sometimes love is not returned, and in this is to be found the tragic dimension of life. He recognizes the need for standards of justice in society and would not fault individuals for claiming what is rightfully theirs. He recognizes that we are constantly dealing with approximations, ambiguities, and compromises in the quest for justice. Essentially, he is taking life as it is as a given with all its complexities, faults, contradictions, dilemmas, difficulties, and puzzles, and using the self-sacrificial life of Jesus as a transcendent ideal by which we measure our individual and collective lives. Secondly, since we are all sinners who constantly fall short of the ideal of *agape*, the main value of this "impossible possibility" in Niebuhr's thought is that it (1) judges us and brings us to repentance and (2) indicates the direction a transformation of life should take. He creates a paradox by combining (a) the recognition that since we fail so miserably to serve our neighbor's good, we are utterly dependent on grace and forgiveness (justification) with (b) a positive hope for progress toward a more holy life and the achievement of justice (sanctification). He holds these two dimensions in dialectical tension so that each corrects the other in a dynamic process with no fixed or final resolution. Hence, given his emphasis on the persistence of sin in the life of the redeemed, the extreme consequences of living a wholly sacrificial life seldom arise except in the rare saint. *Agape* is primarily a judgment on the non-sacrificial life we ordinarily lead, not an ideal likely to be wholeheartedly practiced enough that it threatens to demean the personhood of those who live heedless of their own needs and just claims. Saints may understand self-sacrifice as a vocational hazard voluntarily assumed and thus an expression of their authentic selfhood rather than as a violation of it. Moreover, Jesus himself could exemplify the fullness of sacrificial love only by becoming powerless on the cross, lifted above the complexities, ambiguities, and unavoidable compromises of actual life on this earth. This is a powerful moral perspective.

Niebuhr's interpretation captures much that is central to the Sermon on the Mount and is in keeping with many other New Testament passages (John 15:13, Romans 5:6-11, e.g.). However, self-sacrificial love if consistently practiced is incompatible with civilization, which requires division of labor, assigned roles, duties, rules, accountability, and so on. Only if some sort of stable, organized life is assumed generally can some people be self-sacrificing sometimes. In this sense life could not go on if no one ever insisted that others play their part, share the load, and do their duty. Self-sacrifice cannot serve alone as an ethical guide to any kind of continuing life in a community of people, and Niebuhr never intended it to. He recognized that the social expression of *agape* takes the form of justice in which rational considerations of freedom and equality and the tensions between them come into play. *Agape* itself, in his words, is the "impossible possibility." Nevertheless, by itself self-sacrificing love lacks the element of justice that is essential to any kind of social existence. Justice requires that all persons as persons be regarded as equals and give as well as receive. Sacrificial love requires that only the neighbor matters. The self counts for nothing. For Niebuhr justice arises in the confrontation of love with the complexities of social life. I build it into the basic norm of love itself. Hence, I prefer my interpretation as being closer to what can be rationally defended as a practical basis of ethics in a social setting. I believe that my view is in harmony with much of the spirit and substance of the New Testament, including the teachings and example of Jesus, who did not always insist that everybody all the time sacrifice everything for someone else. In any case, whatever the New Testament meant by *agape*, we need an interpretation of love that is compelling for life in today's world. I make my case on that basis.

Therefore, I contend against Niebuhr that *agape* not be regarded as fundamentally sacrificial in which the self is totally heedless of its own needs and interests as it seeks to serve the neighbor. Love may become sacrificial contextually, but it need not be regarded so in essence. Rather, I propose that *agape* be thought of as mutual love that regards the self and the neighbor as equals in a community of equals, with equal rights, opportunities, responsibilities, and privileges. One who practices *agape* will sacrifice for the neighbor when the neighbor's need exceeds one's own or when the larger good of the community requires it, but likewise will resist appropriately any trespass against the legitimate needs, claims, and interests of the self. Later, I will refine this analysis by distinguishing between the ethical and the ecstatic dimensions of love.

To meet Niebuhr's objection, I propose that *agape* be defined as unconditional mutual love. It does not depend on the response of the neighbor (Matthew 5:43-48). It continues to seek equality, mutuality, and reciprocity, even when the other reacts with hostility or indifference or in a self-seeking way. Unconditional mutual love says, "I will love you on and on no matter what you do, regarding your needs equal to mine and my needs equal to yours." Unconditional mutual love, however, includes an element of justice for the self as well as for others and insists that all count for one and no more than one when goods are to be distributed. The moral ideal is that each person shall have the best life possible within the constraints posed by mutual self-realization. The just and good society will seek to maximize the freedom, well-being, and equality of all citizens consistent with the appropriate limits each imposes on the others. *Agape* seeks a community in which all persons are regarded as equal in worth and deserving of equal consideration.

An ideal community would be made up of citizens devoted to a balance between individual self-fulfillment and the advancement of the common good. It seeks a union of persons in a mutually beneficial, reciprocal relationship among free and equal members. However, inequalities of reward and responsibility may arise contextually, since people differ in ability, merit, and need. Excepting only those based on merit and natural ability, inequalities of power, wealth, and authority are legitimate only as pragmatic adjustments necessary to serve the larger and overriding ideal of a community of free and equal persons ruled by the quest of the best life possible for all. Some inequalities, then, are unavoidable, some are necessary, and some are justifiable. It is hard to improve on the principle that requires from each according to ability and gives to each according to need, while not ignoring merit. Justice and love are apposites that mutually require, limit, and complete each other.

The important point here is two-fold: (1) At the center is an ideal of a community of selves enjoying mutual self-realization joined organically by bonds of unconditional love in which an equality of giving and receiving leads to the highest fulfillment possible for each and all. (2) The sacrificial and the equalitarian elements can be seen as guarding that vital center from either side. The sacrificial dimension of love enters when the larger good of the community or the greater need of some calls for generous and perhaps costly self-giving from others. The equalitarian dimension of love enters when the ideal is threatened by injustice which endangers the rights of the self or others. This model can be illustrated as follows:

The Sacrificial Dimension	Unconditional Mutual Love	The Equalitarian Dimension
Unequal self-giving necessary for the achievement of the highest good of the community and providing for the greater needs of some.	The ideal of mutual self-realization in a community of reciprocal giving and receiving with appropriately assigned duties and benefits.	Equality of rights for self and others instrumental to justice by which each person's claim to self-realization is maintained.

Another way to put this is that at the heart of this ethical vision is an ideal which unites love and justice. Love especially indicates the unbounded self-giving for the sake of the other. Justice especially indicates the worth of every person which establishes freedom to seek self-realization equal to that of the other. In the encounter of self with the neighbor, there is a love element which leads to self-sacrifice, and there is a justice element which leads to equal regard for the self. Informing both is the will to community which generates risk taking and creative initiatives to achieve the ideal of mutual giving and receiving but which is resistant to the destruction or neglect of any. The model can be illustrated as follows:

Love	**The Vital Center**	**Justice**
Sacrifice of self.	Ideal of reciprocal giving and receiving in a community of mutual fulfillment.	Regard for self.

Without the sacrificial element, love runs the risk of falling into a calculation of costs and benefits. This balancing of accounts will neglect the interest of the neighbor and threaten mutuality. Without equal regard for self, love runs the risk of falling into an unjust degradation of self. Love includes a justice element, and justice includes a love element. They coinhere in a unity of apposites.[19]

The procedure is not to begin with abstract principles and then apply them but to start with a given situation as it has developed historically and ask in the light of the ideals of a just and good society what steps would improve society. Working out the requirements of justice in the context of the complexities, tragedies, contradictions, contingencies, and ambiguities of real life will tax the best of minds and make for much conflict among even people of good will, exacerbated by the abounding tendencies toward egocentrism and selfishness, not to mention ignorance, foolishness, and shortsightedness. For society as a whole, the best that can be hoped for is a temporary, workable rough approximation of the norm with many imperfections. I agree with Niebuhr, however, that history presents indeterminate possibilities of good and that no prior limits should be placed on the extent to which justice and the good life may be achieved. The ideal is, as he says, both transcendent to every actual state of affairs and relevant to every situation as judge, guide, and inspiration. As Alfred North Whitehead said, the ethical absolutes of the early Christians were impractical for governing the Roman Empire, but for that very reason these unattainable ideals served as a gauge of the defects of society and thus "spread the infection of an uneasy spirit."

Ethical And Ecstatic Dimensions Of Love

An always troublesome problem for interpreters of the teachings of Jesus is the "hard sayings" of the Sermon on the Mount

(Matthew 5:38-48). Resist not one who is evil. Turn the other cheek if smitten. Go the second mile. Lend to everyone who wants to borrow. Give to beggars. Love your enemies. No fully satisfactory interpretation of these injunctions can be found. A literal exposition will result in harm to oneself or others who are innocent. It lets the bullies, the cheaters, and the violent get away with injustice. Lazy or opportunistic Roman soldiers, of course, loved the literal interpretation of the Sermon on the Mount. Non-literal interpretations run the risk of taking the rigor out of them — watering them down. They are an invitation to taking the offense out of the severe injunctions. I have no perfect resolution to offer that leaves no difficulties. A distinction between an ethical dimension of love and an ecstatic dimension may have some usefulness in this connection, limited though it may be.

Love as an ethical ideal seeks a community based on mutuality and reciprocity in which there is an equality of giving and receiving. Mutual love has a justice element in which every person has an equal claim to fulfillment and an equal duty to be responsible. Ethical love is unconditional and will reach out to others even when they lack merit. But it will resist encroachment upon its own equal claim to fulfillment and will repel if possible any denial of one's own right to be fully human in every respect. Against the pacifist, ethical love would justify killing in self-defense and killing enemies in a just war when non-lethal alternatives are unavailable. They are necessary and tragic emergency means here and now to stop present and ongoing violence. Capital punishment is opposed since the crime has already been committed, and isolation can protect society against future violence.

Love in the ecstatic dimension becomes superethical. In ecstasy one is delirious with impetuous joy in the presence of the beloved and is totally devoted to that person's happiness and well-being. In ecstasy we do not count the cost to ourselves but are totally self-giving, heedless of our own needs. In this mood, sacrifice for the other is not an ethical act of self-denial but the superethical expression of what we most want to do. Ecstasy involves the unpremeditated overflow of boundless affection and the impulsive joy of exhilarating union with the loved one. The ecstatic lover dances with delight in the presence of the beloved. Sensible calculations balancing rights and duties have no place. Rational ethics has been transcended by spiritual ecstasy. Ecstatic love is not an ethical norm. It is a description of how we will act spontaneously in a certain frame of spirit. Love expressed in ecstasy gives all without regard to whether the recipient has any claim on the gift. It is pure grace.

Consider the story of the woman who poured expensive perfume on the head of Jesus (Mark 14:3-9). She was displaying love in the ecstatic dimension. Some present were thinking ethically. They complained that this perfume could have been sold and the proceeds given to the poor. On ethical grounds they were right. What the woman did was indefensible as a moral act. It was irrational and superethical. This deed flowed spontaneously from ecstatic love.

Likewise, the idea of ecstatic love may offer some insight in dealing with the "hard sayings" of the Sermon on the Mount. What on the surface appear as commandments to be obeyed can be usefully seen as a description of how a person in the ecstatic mode will act under certain conditions. They are not imperatives. They are indicatives. They specify not so much what one ought to do but what one will do when in a superethical or ecstatic frame of mind. Not to resist someone who is evil if it would prevent unmerited harm to yourself or harm to others is unethical. Unlimited lending without regard to ability to repay, forgiving seventy times seven, going the second mile, turning the other cheek, letting bullies get away with their meanness or take advantage of those who love without limit is not a basis on which an organized society can exist on a long-term basis. This way of viewing Matthew 5:38-48 is not without problems, but it is better on the whole than any alternative known to me.

Ecstatic love, however, flows at one point into the rational ethical realm. Here it becomes a felt obligation to be self-sacrificial when the larger good of the community requires it or when the neighbor's need is greater than one's own. As I wrote in my *Process Ethics:*

> *The example of Jesus on the cross can be seen as the overflowing of love so great, so rich, so full, so pure that it willingly sacrifices all, even life, itself, for the sake of the beloved. Or it can be seen as a vocational necessity required of Jesus because no lesser means than the sacrifice of life could have been the instrument of salvation for the community. The nature of* agape *is expressed in either interpretation.*[20]

Love has both an ethical and an ecstatic or superethical dimension, and we should not confuse the two. It is quite clear, however, that neither ecstatic nor self-sacrificial ethical *agape* can be the norm of large, impersonal societies. A corporation cannot exist on the basis of forgiving seventy times seven an incompetent employee whose repeated ineptness is costing thousands of dollars. A bank cannot lend money without regard to the ability of the borrower to repay. Ecstasy is not even the mode in which we can live all the time in the most exemplary family life with spouses and children. Ecstatic love is an occasional, fabulous, wonderful overflowing of spectacular affection that adds immeasurably to the joy of life, but it cannot be the day-to-day standard for ordinary life even in the family or the church. We need some rules and a set of defined responsibilities in even the most intimate settings. Love itself carries within itself an element of justice.

Can Christian love in the ethical sense be an appropriate norm for a large, secular, pluralistic, civil society? Can unconditional love for the other that regards the welfare of the neighbor equal with one's own be the ideal expected of the citizens of New York or the United States? Can Americans be expected to sacrifice their own self-interests for their more needy neighbors? Surely, to agree with Reinhold Niebuhr, that would be to hope for an "impossible possibility." Ethical love is a description of ideal life in one-to-one encounters, the family, the church, and other small communities in which unconditional regard for each other can be lived out in face-to-face relationships. Even in these settings, we will often fail, but we can hold it up as the criterion by which we are judged and to which we aspire even in our shortcoming. In this sense, ethical love is the supreme norm that serves as both goal and judge of all achievement in every sphere of life and at every level of society. Realistically, however, we can hope only for some rough approximation with decreasing levels of attainment as we move away from intimate communities toward larger collectives. Nation states cannot be expected, even occasionally, to become ecstatic or self-sacrificing in their devotion to each other! Mutual love, not even to mention sacrificial love, is hardly the guiding rule of relations between General Motors and Toyota, nor does either have aspirations in that direction. We should not expect them to. Ethical love expressed as social policy for large, impersonal societies takes the form of justice. What that norm involves for New York or the United States as secular, pluralistic societies cannot be spelled out here. Pragmatically and politically, of course, Christians have to work within the framework of justice as defined by the secular society in which they have their citizenship and seek to transform it in the light of their own ideals.

Agape And *Eros*

So far I have used the language of *agape* to explain the meaning of Christian love. But what about *eros*? Does it have any positive place in the discussion of Christian ethics? I contend that *eros* is the natural basis for the quest of enjoyment and the quest for universal community. Moreover, it is the ally and counterpart of *agape* when it is properly understood and transformed. *Eros* is the desire to actualize the potential for enjoyment in living beings, the hunger for what satisfies, for what is good for the organism.[21] It has a biological foundation that is to be located in the evolutionary history of life on earth. As Alfred North Whitehead says, all life is driven by a threefold urge "to live, to live well, and to live better."[22]

Inevitably *eros* is self-centered. The newborn baby who seeks food and comfort at the maternal breast loves in return those who love him/her. This natural love between infant and mother extends quickly and easily to father, other family members, and friends, creating reciprocal bonds of support. Another set of natural loves with a more focused bodily erotic component attracts persons of the opposite sex toward each other and forms the basis for the creation of families and the reproduction of life through sexual union. In a minority, physical *eros* attracts persons of the same sex into similar unions with family-forming tendencies. The moral challenge is to extend these natural loves into wider circles of inclusion. The individual is not an isolated self but a bio-social creature organically related to persons biologically and socially, existing in interdependence with nature and other people — a thoroughly relational being. *Eros* drives us toward union with others and creates bonds of love in quest of fulfillment. The self's own good is bound up with the good of others and achieves its own normative ends in communities of mutual support. Beginning with the natural drives that create families and intimate communities in which children are nourished, the ethical challenge is to build upon these natural loves by enlarging the communities with which the self identifies and achieves its own self-realization in bonds of mutual assistance with other members in reciprocal acts of sustenance.

Hence, while *eros* is self-centered, the boundaries of the self can be extended to larger circles of inclusion. Extended communities of interdependent persons can be created in which the good of each is bound up with the good of all, and the good of all is bound up with the good of each. In this light *agape*, Christian love, is not the contrary of *eros*, as the Nygren school of thought contends, but the moralizing of *eros*. *Agape* is the apposite not the opposite of *eros*. It is the universalizing and perfection of the natural loves born in sexual union and nurtured in families to create relationships of mutual support, sympathy, and caring. This desire to meet the needs and advance the interests of all members of a social group — exemplified best in families — is rooted in nature and is the basis for the ethical enlarging of communities united by love.

While perfected, *agape-eros* is universal in principle so that no one is excluded from the community of concern. Nevertheless, the practical fact is that some neighbors are more intimately related to us than others. Family, friends, neighborhood, town, state, nation, and world define communities ever more remote in space and in connections established biologically, socially, and through covenants of mutual support. Love and justice take on different meanings as we move from intimate bonds of association to wider communities of interdependence. No greater challenge to moral wisdom exists than that of determining how our ministries of love are to be distributed among all claimants with needs. While the rule that problems are to be dealt with by the nearest, smallest proficient community possible is a good one, it leaves open what kinds of responsibility we have for those at every level. Needs approach infinity while resources are finite. I cannot out of my own funds provide health insurance for everyone in the whole country, but I can work for national programs that will, even if it costs me more in taxes to do so. I cannot feed every hungry child in Africa or India, but I can contribute to agencies that provide immediate relief. I can support efforts to develop global institutions that make bread, justice, and the means of self-sufficiency available to as many hungry mouths as possible. I can also work for national policies that are generous toward poor countries. International agencies can be created to foster economic development where it is most needed around the planet. Love and the quest for justice express themselves collectively as well in individual acts of kindness. The point is that while we cannot give all to everyone but have to make responsible decisions about how our love is to be apportioned, in principle we cannot be innocently indifferent to any neighbor anywhere.

Eros is a multidimensional and variable energy that is as extensive and broad-ranged as life itself. In human existence it has physical, emotional, and spiritual aspects. It is at one level the desire of the sexes to unite with each other in coitus and companionship. It brings groups together in common enterprises, and it is the urge in individuals for private ecstasy. It is the longing for the true, the good, and the beautiful, and for the vision of God in mystical union. In short, it is the manifestation in all of its forms towards the actualization of the potential given in the genetic materials of every organism at conception. *Eros* may take on a different historical manifestation under given circumstances. Human beings interpret their existence and devise ways of life to express the vital energies present in their bodies and spirits. They organize and direct the drive of life in accordance with their historically-created visions of the true, the good, and the beautiful. Civilizations embody some characteristic *Gestalt,* a pattern of ideals, values, and goals which serve as a normative guide to living. Ethical systems, religions, and philosophies of life lift up possible and recommended ways of directing the drive of life toward fulfillment. *Agape* may be regarded as one of these historically-created visions. As such it embodies a distinctive understanding of human existence before God, and it results in a peculiar style of life which counts the neighbor's need equal to one's own. *Agape* as human love is a spontaneous response to the goodness and grace of God which reproduces toward the neighbor the quality of God's action toward the self.

How, then, do *agape* and *eros* relate to each other? *Eros* is the drive for actualization which is experienced as enjoyment (good). In that sense it is self-centered in seeking the good of a particular organism or self. This gives credence to the definition of *eros* as self-regarding or acquisitive (Nygren) that is so prominent in those theological interpretations that seek to contrast *eros* with *agape.* Its gravitational pull is in the direction of self-actualization, seeking the good of the self in which its energies are present and driving. However, insofar as there is a need for community, a desire for sexual and family relations, a quest for friendship, companionship, common endeavors, and the like, *eros* leads the self toward others in a variety of ways which need not be essentially or exclusively selfish. The energies which urge us toward self-actualization may be sublimated and transformed in an indefinite variety of interactions which may range from simply using others for selfish purposes to the total negation of the self in some act of supreme sacrifice. *Eros,* then, is a variable and complex drive which may unite self-regard and other-regard based simply on its natural and given tendencies. Certainly in sexual relations there are varying degrees of natural affection and ecstatic joy in the presence of the other person. Genetically-rooted erotic urges are not necessarily selfish. Sexual love takes us beyond ourselves toward the other in joyful union in which the partner may be cherished and spontaneously affirmed. Naturally-based human loves may in indeterminate degrees value the neighbor as companion, friend, and fellow sufferer. A sense of mutual need and spontaneous affection based on *eros* itself may unite persons to each other in healthy giving and receiving.

Human intellect, feeling, and imagination can direct, sublimate, transform, and otherwise organize the natural drives of sex and hunger as well as all the other vitalities of human life, including the spiritual quest for union with God. The natural vitality of *eros* may be directed into a wholly self-centered style of relating to others. Or it may be elevated into a quest for universal values and mutual fulfillment in which the other takes an equal place with the self in the good that is sought and shared. *Agape* may be regarded as that transformation or organization of *eros* which, motivated by gratitude to the boundless benevolence of God, reaches out toward the neighbor with unconditional regard. *Agape*, then, is not so much the contrary of *eros* or its negation as it is a possible transformation or organizing principle of *eros*. *Agape* redirects the gravitational pull of *eros* toward self-centered self-actualization so that the human drive for fulfillment is constrained by the love of God manifest in Christ and thus channeled into a way of life which counts the neighbor's good equal to one's own.

If with respect to *agape* the question is whether the love of others excludes love of self, the issue regarding *eros* is whether actualization of the self's potential includes others. Is *eros* irredeemably selfish? Surely, Augustine is right when he claims that the answer depends on the object of *eros*. If the good of the self is sought in what is objectively and absolutely good, namely God, that is in fact salvation. To seek the good of the self in the self is the meaning of sin. So teaches Augustine. I would argue in a similar fashion. If the self is made for community and for fellowship with God, then *eros* which has the Society of God as its aim includes the good of the self in the good of all in which the self shares equally but not selfishly. Self-realization in community is indeed a philosophical statement of the norm of the just and good society which the theological concept of the Society of God requires. In short, when the good sought by the self (*eros*) includes equally the good of the neighbor, it becomes *agape* within that framework. When the process of moralizing, transforming, and perfecting *eros* is complete so that no neighbor is outside the community of persons whose good is sought by the self, *eros* and *agape* become identical.

In short, then, two ways of looking at love come to the same point. *Agape* directs the self to have equal regard for the good of the neighbor. Its distinctive quality is that at its ecstatic heights it is heedless of the interests of the self, although in principle the good of the self is equal to that of the neighbor. *Eros* is the natural drive which, when ethicized, leads the self to seek its good in community with others in the quest of mutual fulfillment. Self-interest is included without being selfish or eliminating the obligation to sacrifice self when the true good of the self and others linked to community welfare is fundamentally threatened.

Using the language of *eros* and *agape*, I have argued that *agape* is other-regarding without negating the self. Transformed or ideal *eros* is self-regarding without negating others. The reason is that the obligation to honor the intrinsic worth of other persons includes permission if not the obligation to honor it in myself. The directive to seek self-realization in community rests on the assumption that the self's real good is social and not private. At their center the good of the self and of the other are on an equal footing. However, at the heights of each, rational calculation gives way to ecstatic spontaneity in which love overflows into sacrificial actions in which cost-counting has no place. *Agape* is a human possibility rooted theologically in the goodness of creation and the *imago dei*. It fulfills the essence or nature with which we are born. We are made for community, for mutuality, for *agape*, in the sense that its realization is the highest good of human life. But its enactment is also an historical achievement in life as the ideal itself is an historical product of the Hebrew-Christian religion. When fully achieved in an individual life, it is experienced as a gift that expresses itself in seeking the good of the neighbor in a community of mutual service. In its ideal form what is divinely commanded is identical with what the self desires. Duty becomes a joyous manifestation of converted character. A good tree brings forth good fruit as its natural product.

The assumption underlying this synthesis is that in God *eros* and *agape* are identical.[23] In the divine life *eros* is the urge toward universal realization or self-realization, that is, the actualization of compossible (logically compatible) ideal ends over time. Since the self-realization of God includes the self-realization of all finite creatures, God's self-love (*eros*) is identical with universal love of the cosmos and all particular individuals within it (*agape*). The *agape* of God spontaneously wills what the *eros* of God naturally desires. *Eros*, as God's self-love, is identical with love of the world and a quest for universal realization and thus is describable as *agape*.[24]

The next chapter will move from a consideration of the principles of Christian ethics to their practice in life.

Endnotes

1. I was profoundly affected decades ago when I looked at a map of the Southern United States that showed nothing but the proportion of blacks and whites in each county. From that one fact alone it was obvious that the higher the proportion of blacks in the county, the greater the resistance of white people to racial change.

2. For an impressive statement by one who does just what I reject, see James W. McClendon, Jr., *Systematic Theology* (Nashville: Abingdon Press, 1986). See also, Stanley Hauerwas, *A Community of Character: Toward a Constructive Christian Social Ethic* (Notre Dame, IN: University of Notre Dame Press, 1981), and *The Peaceable Kingdom: A Primer in Christian Ethics* (Notre Dame, IN: University of Notre Dame Press, 1983). Hauerwas focuses on the church as the focal point of Christian ethics, whereas I am on the boundary between church and world and see the church as playing a role in character formation in a life that is lived out in the world in quest of justice and the extension of the community of those persons for whom justice and the good life are to be sought. He is probably as realistic about actual churches as I am, but he writes for the church that should exist as well as for the very imperfect one that does.

3. The substitution of Society for Kingdom of God is an unsatisfactory compromise between using the sexist and patriarchal terms and any other terms I could think of, all of which were even less adequate.

4. Two books that suggest the rich variety of Christian thinking about ethics are: H. Richard Niebuhr and Waldo Beach, eds., *Christian Ethics: Sources of the Living Tradition* (New York: Ronald Press, 1955), and H. Richard Niebuhr, *Christ and Culture* (New York: Harper & Brothers, 1951).

5. Some of what follows is a revision of material that first appeared in my *Process Ethics: A Constructive System* (Lewiston, NY: Edwin Mellen Press, 1984), 126-36. The Edwin Mellen Press graciously permits its authors to use small portions of books published by them in later works.

6. *The Ethics of Enjoyment* (Atlanta: John Knox Press, 1975).

7. C. H. Dodd, *Gospel and Law* (New York: Cambridge University Press, 1951), 64-83. What follows in the text is my interpretation of Dodd's thesis and should not necessarily be attributed to him.

8. In putting it this way I am trying to incorporate two themes that are sometimes regarded as antithetical: the Society is the gift of God and not a human achievement, but we can participate in its actualization and further its temporal realization by reproducing in our actions the aim and direction of divine activity.

9. Here I reflect the influence of my teacher H. Richard Niebuhr. See his *The Responsible Self* (New York: Harper & Row, 1963).

10. Deontological ethics defines the right in terms of what is required of us by who or what is regarded as morally authoritative (God, law, custom, duty, conscience, intuition, e.g.) without necessary regard to consequences. Teleological ethics defines the right solely by reference to consequences, i.e., by what will achieve the greatest good, as good is understood by the moral agent in question (happiness, pleasure, the Kingdom [Society] of God, e.g.).

11. While certain texts and their implications fit well with this interpretation, I would not want to insist that it is the biblical way of looking at things. Much of the Bible assumes a political model in which God as the Creator-King orders us to act in accordance with divinely-given commands as human kings order their subjects to do certain things. In this framework divine commands are simply imperatives, commands that we must or should obey. I have argued that in our age a biological model would serve us better than a political one.

12. See my *Process Ethics*, 7-36.

13. *Ibid.*, 37-82.

14. For an older but splendid account of the interpretation of *agape* in theological literature, see Gene Outka, *Agape: An Ethical Analysis* (New Haven: Yale University Press, 1972).

15. Reinhold Niebuhr, *An Interpretation of Christian Ethics* (New York: Charles Scribner's Sons, 1935), and Anders Nygren, *Agape and Eros* (London: SPCK, 1957).

16. Paul Ramsey, *Basic Christian Ethics* (New York: Charles Scribner's Sons, 1951), 153-66.

17. Daniel Day Williams, *The Spirit and the Forms of Love* (New York: Harper & Row, 1968), 192-213.

18. Reinhold Niebuhr, *The Nature and Destiny of Man* (New York: Charles Scribner's Sons, 1949), II, 68-97, 244-86; *Faith and History* (New York: Charles Scribner's Sons, 1949), 171-95.

19. Portions of the preceding few paragraphs are taken from my *Process Ethics*, 170-74. Used by permission.

20. *Process Ethics*, 163.

21. Cf. my *Process Ethics*, 180-8.

22. Alfred North Whitehead, *The Function of Reason* (Boston: Beacon Press, 1958), 8.

23. For a fuller discussion, see my *Science, Secularization, and God* (Nashville: Abingdon Press, 1969), 188-94. See also my *Theological Biology: The Case for a New Modernism* (Lewiston, NY: Edwin Mellen Press, 1991), and *Toward a New Modernism* (Lanham, MD: University Press of America, 1997), 77-107.

24. This is a revised and expanded version of a section of my *Process Ethics*, 180-5. Used by permission.

Chapter 6

The Ethics Of Christian Belief: Practice

Stating the principles of New Testament ethics is a legitimate task and serves the necessary purpose of articulating the way the Christian community understands the ends and obligations of life.[1] A perspective on ethics can be compared to other ways of articulating the ideals and norms of morality within and beyond the Christian tradition. It can serve as a useful framework for locating agreement and disagreement and for making alliances to promote this vision of goodness and justice. Reasons can be given for accepting or rejecting this way of believing, acting, and hoping in mutually beneficial conversations. It can be used as a basis for making judgments about right and wrong in matters of personal and social ethics. In short, we need a clear moral vision expressed in principles, norms, and goals. However, this is only part of the task.

Three problems confront us immediately. (1) The first is developing virtuous persons who live out the ethics of love as the spontaneous expression of their character. (2) The second is to ask what it means to live today by the principles of New Testament ethics produced by a much different community in a fundamentally dissimilar setting that assumed the world was about to end. (3) The third is to ask how general principles of love and justice illuminate specific issues and problems we face today. This chapter will take up each of these in turn.

Becoming Loving Persons: The Real Moral Problem

Why don't we love our neighbors as we love ourselves? Christian theology has answered that question with a doctrine of sin. The human condition is that our love is inordinately focused on ourselves rather than directed properly toward God and neighbor. Classical theology has taught that this posture is both universal and chosen. My own understanding combines components from the Augustinian, the Pelagian, and the Irenaean traditions. Three elements of human perversity are worth noting. Here I speak of the norm, the standard paradigm of human existence and its predicament, not taking into account how particular life histories, social location, cultural conditioning, and the realities of race and gender may qualify the generalizations offered.

1. Human beings have an innate hunger for self-fulfillment, a deep inner *eros* that propels them toward the actualization of their potential for enjoyment. Biologically rooted, *eros* extends to every dimension of personhood. It reaches its noblest sublimated heights in the yearning of the spirit for the objectively true, the ultimately excellent, and the intrinsically beautiful. Nevertheless, since it is self-oriented in its basic tendency, the good of the self and of the communities to which the self belongs is intrinsically more attractive than the good of other selves and communities.

2. Natural *eros* is experienced in an atmosphere marked by existential apprehension. The self, mindful of its inescapable freedom, never fully escapes the anxiety generated by the consciousness of finitude and mortality. Although this terror may reside at the fringes of awareness most of the time, there are times in the middle of the night or even at midday when we are suddenly overwhelmed with the unnerving realization that one day we will die.[2] We cannot with certainty achieve the good we desire or avoid the catastrophes of mind and body we fear. We are blessed with the privilege of choice and damned by the frightening necessity of having to choose. Anxiety may entice the self toward egocentric actions to protect and fortify the self and thus to reduce existential terror. Or anxiety may tempt the self to avoid danger by becoming harmless and seeking safe havens away from the storms and strife of life. This response is associated with a failure to confront evil

and injustice — the sin of the timid and the passive. Neither *eros* nor anxiety is sin, but sin arises in the context of both. Their interwoven power constitutes a powerful temptation toward excessive self-regard.

3. In an atmosphere of anxiety, the natural *eros* that drives the self toward its own fulfillment is almost irresistibly magnified by human imagination and choice into inordinate self-concern that distorts the relation of the self to God and others. The transformation of the innate drive toward the good into excessive self-regard goes beyond what the healthy needs of the self require and may produce injustice for other people. Inordinate self-concern may take two forms.

(a) Natural self-centeredness may be transformed into the self-glorification Christian tradition has called spiritual pride, *hubris*. Selfishness and sensuality are its behavioral marks. Self-elevation prompts people to seek pleasure, money, power, material benefits, and psychic gains that tend toward a cherished superior-inferior relationship with others.[3] An anxious self uses its power to attain ends that satisfy the selfish ego and lead to domineering relationships with others that ignore their needs and just claims. Collective aggression arising from *eros* compounded by *hubris* and mixed with anxiety issues forth in the illusive quest for an impregnable security and boundless glory to produce history's great moral evils, as witnessed by the atrocities wrought by the modern nation-state in the twentieth century. The use of power to exploit and subjugate others reaches its most destructive forms in the relations of groups to each other, reaching the acme of horrendous potential in the great empires of ancient and modern times.

(b) The natural self-centeredness of *eros* may take the form of self-depreciation and exaggerated self-protectiveness. This timidity results in an avoidance of responsibility for the self or others or in a failure to actualize the self fully. It may result in a fearful evasion of the duty to resist evil. It may lead to a collaboration with the powerful to secure secondary gains and to minimize threats to the self. Other similar derelictions of duty may follow.

In summary, evil doing is not the product of sheer perversity nor is it necessitated by human nature, although it may be deeply affected by the life histories of selves and communities. Rather the natural bias of *eros* toward self in preference to the neighbor augmented by inordinate self-concern suffused with anxiety constitutes temptation that must be ratified by choice. Ideally, this narcissistic predisposition can be and often is overcome by love that creates an identity with the neighbor, by compassion that reaches out to relieve the suffering of others, and by an intuitive sense of the essential goodness and trustworthiness of life that nurtures tranquility of spirit. Love, compassion, and cosmic trust (faith in God) are likewise primordial human characteristics existing both as natural proclivities and as spiritual achievements. We do right and we do wrong influenced by nature and by deliberate choice. Original evil that produces harm to individuals and social injustice may generate a trajectory of demonic power that extends into future generations to enslave them. This evil outcome begins as a decision in which the fascinating enticement of self-love overwhelms equal or preferential regard for "the other."[4]

The gospel is that in an encounter with the grace of God a transformation of life can occur in which forgiveness is proffered (justification) and a new life of growth toward moral maturity can begin, motivated by the gratitude for the love that turned them around (sanctification). A great deal more would be needed to develop the doctrines of sin and grace. Here I want to assume this background but to enlarge it to speak generally in terms that would apply to human life generally whether or not a specific Christian understanding of sin and salvation is presupposed. My thesis will be that the fundamental problem is not simply that we love ourselves instead of others but that our love is restricted to those nearest and dearest to us by ties of blood, membership, and association. Even here our love is flawed and limited by anxious self-centeredness. Hence, the challenge is twofold: (a) to learn to love everyone better, and (b) to extend the boundaries of concern in the direction of an all-inclusive community in which no one is excluded.

Morally mature persons love their neighbors and seek justice for all as the natural outpouring of their goodness. What we do expresses what we are. In the words of Jesus, a good tree brings forth good fruit. The supreme mission is to nurture loving persons who live out their ideals in practice. Living in accordance with what love requires is what loving persons instinctively do. Virtuous people have formed habits of action that make the good of others equal to their own without being compelled to do so out of a sense of obligation. They act freely and voluntarily. What they are guides what they do. The extent to which moral norms are felt as obligations is the measure of how far we fall short of ideal virtue. Morally mature people experience ethical duties, commandments, laws, imperatives, rules, and the like as descriptions of how they do act, not primarily as prescriptions of how they ought to act. I have already indicated that this is a legitimate way of viewing New Testament ethics. Principles and codes of morality cannot produce virtuous persons who live in conformity with their requirements. They can only describe what virtuous people will do.

The picture we ought to have is not that of a rightly-formed will or conscience bringing behavior into line with principles of moral obligation. It is not a case of reason or will mastering the emotions, the passions, or the lusts of the flesh. It is not a matter of getting people to do what they ought to do in obedience to the moral law as opposed to doing what they want to do in pursuit of self-interest. The issue is not that of the spirit compelling the body to behave in accordance with prescribed duties. Living morally is not the outcome of an internal struggle in which conscience is victorious over contrary desires, impulses, and selfish urges. It is the whole self who acts, not the victor in the war between warring internal factions. Moral character determines moral choice and actions. Immature character, of course, may be internally complex with conflicting passions, values, or beliefs so that a lack of unity may produce moments of indecision, struggle, or inconsistency. Moreover, ambiguous situations arise in which reason can find no alternative that is not a frustrating and unavoidable mixture of good and evil. Nevertheless, virtuous people perform virtuous acts; kind people do kind things. We freely do what is right because we are righteous, naturally do what is just because we are just, voluntarily do what love enjoins because we are loving persons. When our character is properly formed, we want to do as a matter of fact what we ought to do as a matter of principle. Virtues are the patterns of excellence exhibited by the virtuous that flow freely into action, not moral standards that we have to force ourselves to obey. We proceed, then, not by holding up love of neighbor as a norm and demanding compliance by stern acts of will and choice but by asking how we can develop loving persons living in loving families and loving communities. This involves much that is beyond the scope of this chapter.[5]

Nearly everybody loves somebody though nobody loves anybody perfectly or loves everybody. Most people love their immediate family and/or friends. Most nations have friendly relations with some others. At the extreme self-interest may be focused on the isolated self alone. But more frequently our compassion embraces those within groups to which the self belongs and with which the individual identifies, usually for reasons of life history. Love is strong in families and extends to close friends and beyond usually with decreasing intensity. Parents are united in love by sexual bonds and a shared life of intimacy and mutual support. Babies respond to their parents by caring for those who care for them.

The development of a higher morality requires the extension of concern beyond the self and its self-centered communities. Growth in moral virtue extends the natural loves of immediate family, friends, and associates to wider circles of inclusion. It involves enlarging the range of persons for whom compassion is felt, sympathy is shown, whom we will defend, and for whom we will sacrifice if need be. This identification of the self with other is what Richard Rorty calls "solidarity."[6] The aim of moral development is to build character such that the good of others is part of the good we seek for ourselves. The intent is to enlarge self-interest to include others in the community of those in whose good we are interested. The ultimate moral goal is to create a universal community in which no one is left out, marginalized, ignored, or opposed as enemy of the interests of the self.

Communities may be organized and unified by any number of factors individually or in combination. Limits may be set and boundaries drawn on the basis of family, clan, tribe, race, ethnicity, ideology, gender, sexual orientation, ideology, class, history, nationality, culture, and so on. Each of us is related to a whole series of overlapping groupings that join and separate us from others in complex fashion at many levels. I am a white, male, heterosexual, middle class, Baptist, Protestant, Christian American from the South with liberal leanings in theology and politics reared among farmers and textile mill workers — just to make a beginning in outlining all the connections that link and divide me from others. Each one of our memberships creates bonds of sympathy and support with some groupings and corresponding tensions of varying depths, power, and importance with others. Our sundry connections establish a vast array of relationships positive and negative between us and them. They range from sympathy and identity expressed in mutual support to indifference or enmity toward the outsiders. They produce conflicts with consequence extending from trivial to catastrophic. White heterosexual Americans may relate to white homosexual Americans with varying degrees of antipathy extending into violence, while feeling no prejudice to heterosexual black Americans or many other fellow citizens who are different from them in many other respects. Some of the most deeply rooted hatreds and destructive conflicts are found in situations in which the past has produced a demonic power producing bloody strife over generations or centuries — between Hindus and Moslems, Arabs and Jews, Protestants and Catholics in Northern Ireland, tribal rivalries in Africa, and so on. In all of these instances the deepest moral challenge is not to find the right set of obligations to set before the warring factions to which obedience is demanded. It is rather to find ways of breaking down barriers that define the communities with whose good individuals identify with their own. Somehow each has to develop compassion for the other by a mutual sharing of the pain and misery which unites them in a common humanity and destiny. This most commonly occurs when we are led to identify with the suffering of others and to feel it as our own. It is to recognize the stranger and the enemy is a human being just like us with sorrows and joys, fears and hopes like our own. Golda Meir of Israel and Anwar Sadat of Egypt found a common bond and deep motivation in the realization that their grandchildren would have to live with the consequences of their failure to secure peace and justice in the Middle East. Moral progress is made when persons connect their own good with the good of others previously excluded from the community of common concern, mutual support, and reciprocal sympathy.

The first challenge in moving from theory to practice, then, is to extend our natural loves driven by *eros* until they are ethicized by including all persons in the community of neighbors who are loved, at which point *eros* is identical with *agape*. In the universal community in which the good of others is included in the good in which the self is interested, *eros* and *agape* are one in human beings as they are in God. Love cannot be commanded. At any given point, we either love someone, or we do not. Meeting our moral obligation, then, is not a matter of putting self-interest under the command of the will and forcing the self to take the good of others into account. It is rather extending our natural *eros*-based loves until all our neighbors are included. In this universal community, we will not need to be commanded to love but will love as the spontaneous expression of our moral character, as the natural outpouring of who we are as loving beings. This analysis comports well with New Testament ethics in which believers love God and even undeserving neighbors because they have first been loved. They forgive others as they have been forgiven. Our self-centered *eros* focused on our own good becomes moralized as we begin to love those who love us and include their good in the good we naturally seek.

The problem is that limits are established and boundaries are drawn separating "us" from "them" long before universality is achieved. Unless babies are loved from the beginning and nurtured in an environment in which they are cared for, the process has little chance of beginning. Even when love is present in the family, boundaries get drawn within the life history of children as they appropriate patterns of behavior modeled for them by parents and absorb values from the wider culture. The "others" outside the community of love may be excluded for all sorts of reasons — race, region, religion, nationality, class, sexual orientation, ethnic and cultural considerations, and so on. We may be united to others by race and separated by class or religion and so on. We are all subject to demonic influences from the past that get incorporated into social practices and personality structure in ways that poison relationships. Parents and children may be beset by jealousies, rivalries, competition for attention, and other factors that fracture community within families. Love and hatred may be most powerful in families due to the intensity of feelings and the depth of intimate relationships. The healthy development of children may be hindered by destructive patterns of behavior in their parents. The children may then reproduce them in their own child-rearing practices, creating a persistent chain of pernicious inheritance over many generations. Even the best of families may be crippled by ruinous habits and distorted personality structures. Demonic configurations may be rooted deeply in generations past. Love is seldom perfect, and community is less than ideal even in the most intimate relationships.

Ideals held by communities themselves may, of course, be perverted and require transformation. Long-standing moral traditions may be perverse out of ignorance, the selfishness of ruling classes, the blind emotions of the masses, or bondage to the past. Progress may be inhibited by the simple failure of imagination to grasp ideals more productive of enjoyment, justice, and the fulfillment of human potential. Whole cultures are poisoned by factors that have a long history, as is evidenced by the conflicts in the Middle East and the ethnic wars of Africa. White children in the American South for generations grew up internalizing the caste system that perpetuated segregation and other forms of racial injustice with horrible components of violence. Moral growth is stunted in most of us long before the mature level of inclusion in a universal community is achieved. The challenge is to break down the barriers that limit our love to our kind, the "we" and the "us" who stand over against the rest. This does not necessarily involve active enmity and usually does not except where conflicts over mutually-desired goods or contests over competing ideologies and values precipitate a battle that ends with winners and losers. Usually it simply means indifference and neglect of the needs of the excluded "others" or of those who are simply far away and whose cries of distress can be avoided. A hungry child at our doorstep usually evokes a different response from the starving child thousands of miles away known only by a picture on television or noted in a newspaper.

Simply holding up norms of obligation is not commonly effective in changing behavior. Usually what does is some experience in which the pain or need of the other becomes so real to us that we identify with it and feel it as our own. When enough Israelis weep for the sorrows and injustices experienced by Palestinians in exile, and when enough Arabs mourn because of centuries of Jewish suffering and homelessness, then peace with justice will have a chance. Lacking that, compromises arising from mere negotiation may produce a shallow accommodation that is likely to be unstable. Changes of attitude on race or sexual orientation most often come about when people come for whatever reason to an awareness of the hurt and devastation that destructive attitudes, values, and actions have in crippling and crushing innocent lives who need and deserve better treatment. Moral progress is made by increasing our sensitivity to the distress, misery, and affliction of the excluded others through experience and imagination. What happens is more like coming to feel sympathy and compassion for those in need rather than acknowledging our duty to obey newly adopted moral norms.[7]

To conclude, a moral tradition defines norms and obligations peculiar to itself. I have outlined a version of New Testament ethics embodied in the Christian community. The main point, however, is that we do not produce persons who live out the moral creed by holding up imperatives and goals and demanding conformity. Rather we produce virtuous persons by nurturing and modeling the normative life in families and larger communities so that they develop the character that will issue forth in practices that express the professed ideals. In Christian ethics this means creating a process by which the natural loves rooted in *eros* that seeks a good centered initially in the self and family are transformed into the *agape* that regards as neighbor all who belong to the human community. Ideally, children grow up knowing they are loved by God and by all in the intimate communities surrounding them. In such a setting, the deep awareness of being loved evokes a responsive love toward God and others that ideally never stops enlarging the circle until no one is left outside the community of mutual care. In this universal moral society, each naturally seeks the good of all, and all spontaneously seek the good of each. To the extent that the process works, imperatives defining what we ought to do become descriptions of what we actually will do. Obligations become not burdens to be imposed on a recalcitrant non-moral self but indications of how morally mature persons behave. The extent to which we fail to reach the highest level of excellence in character and virtue defines our moral failure. The realism of the Book of Romans, of Augustine, Calvin, and their contemporary disciples, which I share, leads us to expect that self-centeredness and limited loves are deep, persistent, and never more than partially overcome in the lives of the best of societies and the most saintly of individuals. The norms and goals of the universal community uniting each and all in bonds of mutual love stand before us as always to challenge, judge, and motivate us to ever higher levels of achievement of justice and joy and thus to "spread the infection of an uneasy spirit."

The Role Of Churches

Churches have the potential for playing an important role in the process of training virtuous persons and extending the bonds and boundaries of community. Denominations and congregations vary so much in every respect that no generalization about what they actually do is fully accurate. Ideally, they are societies united by their love of God and of each other who seek to "increase the love of God and neighbor" in the world.[8] At their best they exemplify in their own life what a good community is. Most of them are quite good at this in times of personal and family crisis when members and ministers gather around to meet needs and to comfort. These ministries to each other occur in significant ways in widely varying circumstances. This despite the fact that in many urban churches members see each other only on Sunday and in other congregational meetings so that the ties of intimacy and mutual assistance are limited. Churches train children in the virtues of kindness and helpfulness. Most also engage in ministries of mercy beyond themselves through money and services rendered in voluntary organizations in feeding the hungry and meeting other needs of the body and soul. Some are prophetic and challenge prevailing patterns of injustice in society as a whole.

Churches are generally not as successful in breaking down walls of prejudice and hostility among outsiders unlike them. Most simply reflect the cultural values of their members and the ideologies associated with their class and social location. Denominations whose majority membership is made up of the successful and well-off cannot be expected to be pioneers of radical social transformation. Churches of the marginalized may offer hope of a blessed life beyond, while adjusting as best they can to the harsh realities of this one that cause them to suffer. Or they may seek to exemplify radical ideals of community in their own internal life and either count that as their contribution to society or use their own base as the launching pad of a revolutionary movement to remake society. Churches with broadly distributed membership can be counted on to preserve and defend the best of achieved social values and to be proponents of moderate and gradual changes that benefit those on the margins and at the bottom. Churches tend to reflect the larger divisions of society within their own rank, mirroring worldly hierarchies of race, class, nationality, gender, and sexual orientation.[9]

To their shame they have blessed nearly every evil and injustice we can name and often lag behind secular society in moral progress. They should be the first, and sometimes are, but may be the last to turn a sensitive ear to the cries of the poor and oppressed. In the American Civil War and in two World Wars in the twentieth century, Christians killed each other on fields of battle and dropped bombs on enemy cities containing many who loved Jesus as much as they. For centuries Christians persecuted Jews, and many churches supported Hitler or at least did not seriously object to his nefarious schemes. After being treated violently themselves for the first few centuries, Christians in turn used the power of the sword to exterminate heretics. The Christian past in many ways is an ugly picture. Churches are as ambiguous in their values, practices, and influence as are other institutions, large and small. Frequently disciples of Jesus obstruct the extension of love toward wider circles of inclusion and mutual service. Most churches are a hindrance rather than a help to the full acceptance of gays and lesbians, usually marking them out for special notice as sinners.

Nevertheless, they have an important role to play in creating persons of excellent virtue, forming mature moral character, and extending the bonds of love to the strangers and wayfarers of the land. They are already to some extent and can become more effective instruments of serving the neighbor who is in need of bread, justice, and warm embrace. They do and could do better in ministering to the weak, the oppressed, and the wretched of the earth. They have by their nature and purpose the potential of breaking down walls of hostility and extending the boundaries of community within which all are devoted to the common good and the good of each. The church is one of the few institutions, paralleled only by those of other ethically-based religious faiths, whose central purpose is to increase the love of God and love of neighbor. In that foundation is great potential for developing virtuous persons of mature moral character who care for each and all in a community of mutual service. The task is to develop that potential by delivering actual churches from their many idolatries and limited loves.

As important as the role of churches may be, however, they are not the only channels through which increase in goodness occurs. Secular processes may change the cultural consciousness for the better over periods of time. Churches may lead but often follow and sometimes resist these trends. The ideals of freedom, equality, and justice for all expressed in the founding documents of this country marked an admirable advance over the past. The Jewish-Christian tradition was one source of these principles, but they also were developed by the philosophers of the Enlightenment who were in part rebels against it. The extension of these ideals leading to the overthrow of slavery, the emancipation of women, and now to greater acceptance of gays and lesbians has been the work of pioneers inside and outside the churches.

God works through the *eros* that drives all of life toward its highest fulfillment. The moralizing and perfection of this drive is a process that can occur anywhere on earth. It takes place whenever human compassion and imagination lead to ideals and actions that reach out to include the good of others as part of the good we seek for ourselves. One place this tendency developed with peculiar efficacy and consequence on this planet was in the history of Israel and in Jesus of Nazareth. The demand for justice found in the prophets of the Old Testament has had influence far beyond the biblical tradition. It expressed itself in the wrath of that atheist Jew Karl Marx, who was outraged at the oppression of working people in the exploding capitalistic economy. The move to include the good of others previously excluded takes place outside and in opposition to churches. Nevertheless, the *agape* of God expounded in the New Testament that leads to a responsive reproduction of *agape* in our relations to others is a powerful force in history which continues to express itself in the message and ministry of churches.

The Compatibility Of Christianity With Civilization

The first step in moving from the theory of Christian ethics toward practice is to produce loving persons. A second challenge is equally formidable. The world in which Christianity was born is very different from the setting in which contemporary churches and disciples of Jesus find themselves. How can this original vision guide us today? My thesis is that New Testament Christianity is incompatible with civilization and that we face a difficult task in preserving what is valid in that original vision in circumstances never contemplated by the early church. If we lived by the radical ethic at the heart of the New Testament, we would have homeless people living with us as long as anyone was without a place to live. We would not spend money on any non-essential item until every hungry person was fed. Anything less than that is a compromise. It may be a necessary compromise, and it may be a justifiable compromise. But that it is a compromise, I have no doubt.

New Testament Christians lived in the expectation that the world would end soon. Jesus said the final hour of judgment and redemption would occur in the lifetime of some presently living (Matthew 10:23, 16:27-28; Mark 8:38—39:1, 13:30, 14:61-62).[10] Similar expectations appear throughout the New Testament (Romans 13:12; Philippians 4:5; 1 Thessalonians 4:17; James 5:8; 1 John 2:18; 1 Peter 4:7; Revelation 1:1-3, 22:10-20). Since the End was so near, Paul urged everyone to remain in his present state, whether married or unmarried, slave or free, and noted that ordinary worldly affairs didn't matter much in view of the impending crisis (1 Corinthians 7:24-31). Interpreters from the beginning have tried to find ways to rescue Jesus, Paul, and the New Testament generally from this error.[11] One of the earliest was the author of 2 Peter who had to contend with the skeptics who taunted believers with the fact that the promised return of Jesus had not occurred, reminding them that things have continued as they were from the beginning of creation (3:3-10).

In light of the expectation that the world will end very shortly, even within the lifetime of some now living, the most urgent necessity was to get and stay prepared for the coming judgment and redemption by living now in anticipation of what was about to happen (Mark 1:15). Preserving and reforming the institutions of secular society was of no concern, since "the form of this world is passing away" (1 Corinthians 7:31 RSV). In any case, by and large the earliest Christians were a small sect from the lower socio-economic classes with little power to influence the basic social order around them in the short term (Cf. 1 Corinthians 1:26).[12]

In addition to the apocalyptic expectation that gripped New Testament Christians, we have to deal with those "hard sayings" of Jesus in the Sermon on the Mount (Matthew 5:38-43). Resist not one who is evil. Lend to every one who would borrow. Give to every beggar. Go the second mile. Not only are murder and adultery wrong, but so are anger, hatred, and lustful looks. We must love enemies, avoid worry about tomorrow, and, in short, be perfect, just like God (Matthew 5-6). Some have suggested that these stringent imperatives indicate how we ought to live given the fact that this world is in its last days, thus canceling ordinary rules and responsibilities. Others say that these mandates tell us what we should do when confronted by a solitary neighbor. All other people have for that moment been removed from consideration. In such a situation we are to serve that one person in absolute sacrificial devotion, completely ignoring our own needs and just claims. In real life, of course, there are always many neighbors, making it necessary to devise a theory about how to distribute our love appropriately. A standard Protestant interpretation is that the Sermon on the Mount shows that we stand condemned by the moral law, leading us to flee in repentance to grace as our only hope.

Whether or not any one of these interpretations captures what Jesus had in mind, the "hard sayings" certainly are impractical for organizing daily life and carrying on the routines of commerce. Every prudent move to preserve one's own life and well-being is cast aside by the injunction that we are to be totally devoted to the service of our neighbors, heedless of our own interests. Christians have demonstrated remarkable creativity in showing that Jesus did not mean these injunctions to be taken literally, that he did not really intend for us to do what he commanded. Despite the warning of Jesus, we are constantly relaxing not only the least but also some of the biggest demands (Matthew 5:19). An instance in which most Christians simply ignore completely what Jesus commanded his disciples to do is found in Matthew 10:8. Jesus charges his disciples to cast out demons and raise the dead. Churches generally assert that we are to continue the ministry of the Apostles. However, I know of no churches whatsoever that have a ministry of raising the dead and very few that cast out demons. If we were Christians in the New Testament sense, we would do both in obedience to what Jesus plainly said.

Finally, we cannot escape the implications of a simple principle. Jesus urged that we love our neighbor as we love ourselves (Luke 10:25-28; see also, Romans 12:8-10; Galatians 5:14; James 2:8). We seldom meditate for long on the drastic implications of that simple injunction. This commandment can be interpreted in a minimal or equalitarian sense (neighbor and self held in equal regard) or in a maximal or sacrificial sense (neighbor takes preference over self). Christian love (*agape*) minimally requires that we count everyone else's good equal to our own. Maximally it requires that we totally sacrifice our own interests in order to serve others (Jesus on the cross, Romans 5:8, Matthew 5:38-43). In that sacrificial frame of mind we do not protect, even non-violently, our legitimate self-interests against the aggression of evildoers (Matthew 5:38) or against those who cannot or will not pay their debts to us

(Matthew 5:42). Under either the minimal or the maximal interpretation, the love commandment, if taken seriously and literally, would mean that whenever I confront someone whose need is greater than my own, I must give to her/him and all others so situated until I am no better off than the neediest person on earth.[13]

I conclude that the love ethic at the center of the New Testament is incompatible with civilization. The incongruity is nearly total when love is interpreted in the maximal or sacrificial sense but is great when love of neighbor as oneself is seen in the minimal or equalitarian sense. Total self-giving love that demands nothing from the other is irreconcilable with assigned roles, duties, division of labor, accountability, and so on. When people are starving, love does not invest in scientific research that will in time discover that our universe began with a "big bang" and offer various opinions as to how fast it is expanding. Nor would it support professors who write articles about the incompatibility of Christianity with civilization. Its absolute ideals cannot without dilution be harmonized with the rules and requirements of organized life in society extended over many generations. The unqualified demands of sacrificial love require their implementation in the moment without regard for future consequences for self or others. Orderly life could not go on if no one ever insisted that others play their part, share the load, live by the rules of civilized society, and carry out their obligations. A corporation cannot forgive seventy times seven times an incompetent employee whose constant mistakes are costing thousands of dollars (Matthew 18:22). Society would be in chaos if no one restrained evildoers and prevented them from oppressing or killing the weak and innocent. Justice requires that rules of fairness be enforced, coercively if necessary. Total non-resistance to evildoers would make justice impossible. The absolute and unrestrained impulses of pure love overflow all boundaries, ignore all rules, and disregard all but the immediate need before it to which it ministers without holding anything back for another occasion or another neighbor. Unrestrained love does not save for a rainy day. It gives all here and now to whoever needs it. Civilization cannot be built on such foundations.

The *agape* ethic at the heart of the New Testament can best be lived out in small intimate communities. However, even when face to face, personal interactions among people are possible and dominant, the love ethic requires adaptations and some rules. As we move into larger societies, even more drastic compromises are necessary, inevitable, and justified. When we are talking about the relationship of nations to each other, we may wonder if the requirement that we regard the other party's good equal to our own has become totally irrelevant! The notion that one nation should sacrifice its welfare for the welfare of the other is not even on the agenda. Repeatedly we are told by our leaders that national self-interest is the supreme rule of foreign policy.

Of what value, then, is New Testament Christianity for today? Alfred North Whitehead has put it as well as anyone. The impractical ideals of the first century are a standard by which to measure the shortcomings of society. "So long as the Galilean images are but the dreams of an unrealized world, so long they must spread the infection of an uneasy spirit."[14] This does not refer to the evocation of guilt but to an awareness of the gap between what is and what could be, at least in terms of a closer approximation. A morally serious person of faith cannot take *agape* seriously and be at ease with any status quo. Reinhold Niebuhr made the same point. *Agape*, Christian love, is an "impossible possibility." Nevertheless, it is relevant in all situations as both judge of every present achievement and guide to further moral advance.

If there is to be an ongoing civilization organized into institutions (family, school, state, corporations, and the like) in which we assume responsibility for preserving the traditions and achievements of the past, then the *agape* love ethic at the core of the New Testament must be severely compromised. Our failure is not that we make the compromises that make civilization possible but that *we make them long before they are necessary*. After all, if enough Americans were committed to doing so, we could through governmental action and voluntary private efforts see to it that every person in this country had a place to live, food to eat, medical insurance, and enough resources to live decently. It would be costly to most of us and would require the sacrifice of advantages we now complacently enjoy. But it might contribute to our spiritual health.

This brief summary obscures the fact that the New Testament is a complex book with many strands, multiple themes, and contrasting theological perspectives reflecting varying circumstances in the primitive church. Not all of them can be harmonized with each other or with the perspective I have offered here. In particular, we cannot assume that every ethical passage in the New Testament is controlled by either apocalyptic fervor or by the ethics of equalitarian or sacrificial love in its most radical form. Every interpretation that yearns for unity and consistency must of necessity select certain themes as crucial and interpret everything else in that light. My only claim is that my scheme is not without defense, even if not free from difficulties. The New Testament can legitimately be interpreted in other ways, of course. I merely contend that every alternative to my interpretation of the core New Testament ethic will encounter formidable, if not equally grave, difficulties created by the variety of perspectives within the text itself.

New Testament Christians obviously had to accommodate themselves to the world as it was while it lasted. The following examples indicate some of the ways they came to terms with the values and institutions of the world they inhabited.

1. Slavery is accepted, and slaves are urged to obey their masters with a glad heart (Ephesians 6:5-6; Colossians 3:22; 1 Timothy 6:1-2; Titus 2:9; 1 Peter 2:18-19; Philemon). Even if the treatment of slaves would be improved by these admonitions as contrasted with typical contemporary practices, the fact remains that slavery as such is not attacked.

2. Women are subordinated to men, and their roles limited. In particular, they are urged to be submissive to their husbands, to keep silent in the church, and forbidden to teach or have authority over men (1 Corinthians 11:1-12, 14:34; Ephesians 5:22-23; Colossians 3:18; 1 Timothy 2:11-14; Titus 2:5; 1 Peter 3:1). Even if these texts do transform and improve current practices in some ways, the fact remains that they teach a subservient role for women.

With respect to both slavery and the inferior role assigned to women, we have to ask whether some biblical writers simply accepted both without question as compatible with love. Or were they making necessary and appropriate accommodation to current institutions in light of the circumstances and the imminent end of the age? Was the subservient status of women and slaves so deeply rooted in the traditions of that time that even those imbued with the ethics of love saw no fundamental contradiction with the prevailing institutional framework? Granted that the New Testament requires that women and slaves be treated with gentleness, kindness, and compassion, was it assumed that love required no condemnation of slavery and the subornation of slaves and women as such? If the answer is yes, then we have to say that in our opinion this represented a failure to see the full implication of what was central to their own thinking.

3. Obedience to the state is sometimes unconditionally and uncritically demanded (Titus 3:1; 1 Peter 2:13-14). Paul says that God has instituted the state to execute wrath on wrongdoers. This implies that if the ruling authorities demand it, Christians should participate in the violence the state employs while punishing evildoers (Romans 13:1-7). This is hard to reconcile with Matthew 5:38. The state does not always execute wrath on evildoers. Sometimes it persecutes the righteous, as noted in the New Testament itself. State governments in the South where I grew up were often a threat to those seeking racial justice and sometimes broke the bones of union organizers and members who struggled against powerful corporations for better wages and working conditions.

These perspectives can be viewed in at least five different ways or in various combinations:
1. The interim is so short that worldly institutions and the usual arrangements of family, state, and society are of little importance. Hence, one can simply adapt to them as needed or necessary but modifying them where possible in the light of Christian principles.
2. They are necessary or acceptable compromises with the current social order, since it is impossible to live literally by *agape* in any organized society.

3. Some ethical prescriptions reflect cultural values of that time and place. Under strict scrutiny they appear to be in conflict with what we understand the love ethic to imply and require.
4. Love, salvation, freedom, equality, and the like are inward, spiritual matters and have no necessary implications for outward, worldly relationships, institutions, and practices. In this light, e.g., Galatians 3:28 is not in necessary conflict with 1 Corinthians 7:21-31, 14:34 and numerous other passages in which hierarchy and subordination are approved or mandated.[15]
5. The demanding love ethic applies only within the church but not to secular society, e.g., Matthew 18:22.

Christians have come to terms with the world in many ways as they have wrestled with the relationship between the high, even impossible, ideals of the New Testament and the realities, necessities, complexities, and ambiguities of actual life in sinful society. These controversies rage whether or not the end of the world is expected momentarily. Consider as a start the following: the debates between pacifists and just war proponents, between slaveholders and abolitionists, segregationists and integrationists, feminists and traditionalists, monarchists and democrats, hierarchalists and egalitarians, defenders of wealth and proponents of equal distribution, defenders of order justifying repression and proponents of justice demanding freedom and equality, and on and on. Christian natural law theorists for centuries distinguished between an Edenic age in which freedom, equality, peace, and righteousness were the norm and the post-Edenic age in which hierarchy, the rule of some over others, the use of coercion to restrain sin, and even slavery and war are necessary, justifiable, or unavoidable. Leaving aside all the many instances in which the disputants were, not dishonestly but in effect, devising self-serving theories to defend their narrow interests rather than seeking an impartial justice, we have to admit that the problems are indeed difficult and yield no obvious solutions. Few proposals are free of shortcomings when measured by some New Testament texts or the facts of the matter. Nearly every position taken on these and all other matters could be supported by something in the Bible. Few interpreters shy away from claiming that their interpretation is the real biblical view and the one most in tune with Jesus himself.[16]

Love And Civilization

Can more be said about how love can serve as a norm in a complex society with enduring institutions, a division of labor, assigned roles, family responsibilities, nation-states, governments of law, and ideals of justice? Can love be made compatible with civilization expected to last indefinitely?

The norm of Christian love taken literally implies that whenever I am confronted with a need greater than my own, I am called upon to sacrifice my own interest in an effort to meet it.[17] Such a view strictly insisted upon might be called fanatical, unrelenting, and oppressive. A similar charge has been made against act utilitarianism. If one is obligated in every moral situation to do what maximizes general or universal welfare, then little freedom for self-actualization is left. Every act is momentous. No finite set of obligations can ever be discharged so that one can say that duty has been done. Immanuel Kant made this observation the basis of an argument for immortality. Similarly, the love ethic of the New Testament seems to generate a similar agenda of impossible demands so that the self is smothered under an unbearable burden. Surprisingly, most Christians seem remarkably untroubled by this and easily identify their relatively complacent and comfortable lives with Christian discipleship as long as they are church-going, law-abiding citizens who live decent lives doing some good and no deliberate harm to others. Nevertheless, a serious reading of the New Testament forces us to ask whether it is possible to reconcile its radical ethic with a life of adventure and joy in quest of creative self-actualization. Can one enter into a career of robust enjoyment, seeking the full and zestful actualization of all the rich variety of human pleasures, satisfactions, and accomplishments and still be a morally responsible person? Or does one have a choice between the joyful pursuit of self-actualization and burdensome moral duty to the poor and oppressed and needy who are always with us?

This is probably the greatest dilemma of an *agape* ethic. Life was given to be enjoyed, and yet in the midst of so much misery can one be happy in one's own success and enjoyment? A theology of creation points one way, while the recognition of injustice and evil leads in the opposite direction. The victory of grace over law seems the most promising theological approach by which one may preserve the integrity of moral obligation and yet live in joyful gratitude, free to be and to enjoy life as an accepted and acceptable child of God. Yet, in Niebuhr's terms, where does the possible that I can and ought to do become the impossible that I cannot morally and factually accomplish? However much one may appeal to the grace which covers all our sins and frees us to live in serenity and joy in pursuit of reasonable pleasures for ourselves, the tension which calls us into a ministry to suffering people remains. Some neighbor somewhere is always worse off than myself.

Is there any alternative but to mark out a clearing under the umbrella of grace where we can pursue life with joyful abandon in an adventurous quest of the richest and fullest possible enjoyments? Claiming such space is grounded in the created goodness and inherent worth of one's own life given and acknowledged by God. It is permissible and necessary because of our sheer finiteness and our limited responsibility for causing and curing the tragedy and misery which preceded us and now surrounds us. This recognition frees us from the unbearable burden of taking all the world's ills upon ourselves. Life in grace is freedom to be, to enjoy, to pursue happiness within one's own space. Else what good is forgiveness for sin if life is perpetually weighted down by the enslaving power of unrelenting moral obligation? Surely part of the liberating work of grace is freedom from the bondage of infinite moral duty! My argument, however, is that justice and merit themselves create some circle around us in which we can have a life of our own in pursuit of our own self-realization.

Yet the task of relating grace to law is never done. How large a space shall we claim? What are the boundaries of this freedom to be ourselves in a zestful quest of our own self-actualization? How far shall we distance ourselves from the anguished cries of hungry children? How far shall we go in benign neglect in avoiding responsibility for relieving the misery of our neighbors that grace may abound? Where does the gift of grace end and the demand for obedience to the heavenly vision begin?

Perhaps no more can be said than that the dialectic of grace and law becomes operational in human life in the tension between complacency and despair. Those who are enslaved by the despair of never being able to complete the moral task of loving others need to hear the freeing word of grace which clears them out a space to live and be in peace. Those who are busy with their own selfish preoccupations or at ease in Zion in the complacency of cheap and misunderstood grace need to hear the demand to be about the business of meeting the needs of those who suffer. The gift of grace frees us from despair. The demand of the law undercuts complacency. Life is lived in responsible freedom between these poles in the creative tension that preserves our space without setting up an inviolable territory of selfish preoccupation. The other dialectic is that related to growth in grace toward Christian maturity by which obligation is transformed into free, grateful, and spontaneous loving in which what we do expresses what we have become. The process never ends and the questions are never fully answered. Nevertheless, in the interplay between grace and law, one may find a way to combine a zestful quest for joy abundant and a life of moral responsibility in a continuing quest of maturity.

Beyond establishing this basic orientation, some additional comments further clarify the implications of a sacrificial-equalitarian ethic for individual responsibility and public policy. The fact is that unless I belong to the very worst-off group in society, there are always many neighbors whose need greatly exceeds my own. Does this mean that I can never proceed to better my own condition as long as any person is less well off than myself? Can I never provide music lessons or a college education for my children while a neighbor's offspring lack food and shelter? Would a society devoted to Christian principles never build a park or tennis court while some of its members were starving? It would appear that *agape* as the principle of life for individuals in society results in acts and policies strictly oriented to serving the worst-off groups in society.

The consequence would be a one-way vector which would direct moral action toward those with the greatest deprivation. The implication is a leveling off at the lowest level of human fulfillment. Equality for all before excellence for any is the outcome of unqualified love. It can certainly be said that *agape* does create a bias and direction which favors the claims of the neediest. Yet it cannot be said that all moral action without exception is to be guided by an absolute equalitarian policy. Some of the factors which must be taken into account can only be listed.

First, there is the tension between seeking the fulfillment of the nearest with less deprivation and the neediest who may be far away. The nearest not only includes those in geographical proximity but those close neighbors for whom we have a special responsibility given our chosen roles and our natural destiny. We have immediate responsibilities as parents, spouses, and children, for example. A full account of duty would include a vocational ethic specifying our responsibilities in these naturally occurring lots as well as in the offices and roles we play as workers and citizens in society. Finally, there are those shared commitments we have in the voluntary associations to which we belong in pursuit of the common good and social justice.

Second, there is the tension between the essential needs of survival, security, and health and those enriching values that add quality and breadth to welfare. Food is essential to life but good music may add great meaning and joy. Sometimes the latter benefit for some must be purchased at the expense of the former for others. To take a simple (and inadequate) example, a rich benefactor might face the choice between endowing a symphony orchestra and giving an equal amount to relieve immediate starvation in Africa. (This assumes the problematic fact that in a society guided by *agape* there would be rich benefactors!)

Third, tension arises between short-term and long-term investments in human welfare. The same benefactor might choose between giving a million dollars to buy food in the midst of a famine in Ethiopia or sponsoring a rural agricultural development project in Bangladesh that would not have a pay-off for nearly a decade.

Fourth, qualifications are introduced by the principle of merit, achievement, and effort. The New Testament itself contains the admonition that those who do not work do not eat (2 Thessalonians 3:6-12). Love does not pamper the lazy but when appropriate insists on a principle of justice in which each receives in accordance with contribution or merit.

Finally, those who are well off are under most obligation to be generous, even to sacrifice, in order to meet the fundamental needs of their neighbors that are essential to life. Beyond that we are under less constraint to seek the equality of all in all respects pertaining to income and wealth. Yet the line between needs and wants or between what is necessary for well-being and what would merely provide an enrichment of life is hard to draw. It is impossible to quantify or to make precise judgments in these matters.

Love cannot do its proper work without the assistance of creative imagination and intelligent weighing of competing claims. It must make many compromises and endure many trade-offs in its attempt to weave the tangled threads of human possibility and need into a tapestry exhibiting the greatest harmony and richest fulfillment of the whole community of individuals. Love stands beyond most human achievements as a lure and demand for a more ideal organization of human interactions that would be more creative and more fulfilling than the status quo. It demands more and better from us in behalf of others than our selfish preoccupations and skillful rationalizations of our own interests generally produce. The heights of sacrificial-equalitarian love are seldom reached except in a few saints or in occasional moments of intimate interaction with those nearest and dearest to us. *Agape* draws us away from ourselves to the neighbor's good. Love is a principle of continuing transformation in the lives of those open to its influence and imperatives. It never lets us go. But creative intelligence must guide its generous and overflowing bounty of other-directed beneficence that obstruct ideal harmonies and perfect fulfillment of all.

Love And Civilization: A Final Revisiting

As I was writing this chapter, I came across an article by the Australian philosopher Peter Singer, now teaching at Princeton

University, that posed the questions all over again in a startling way.[18] He gives some imaginary examples of people who act selfishly in a situation that results in the death of a child. One story will do. Bob has invested most of his savings in a rare and costly car, a Bugatti, that he has not been able to insure.[19] He enjoys the car and expects that it will increase in value over the years and provide him with added savings for his retirement. One day he parks the car near the end of a railroad siding and goes for a walk. He sees a runaway train coming down the tracks. Further down the tracks is a child who will be killed if something is not done. Bob cannot stop the train, and the child is too far away for a warning to be heard. But he could throw a switch that will send the car down another track, the one where his Bugatti is parked. That way nobody will be killed, but the car will be totally wrecked. Bob decides not to throw the switch, and the child is killed. He lives comfortably for many years, sells the Bugatti for a good profit, and has a prosperous retirement.

Had Bob made a sacrifice, a life could have been saved then and there in full view. We all condemn his actions. How could he not deny himself something he could get along without when someone dies on the spot as a result? Singer goes on to point out that when we spend money on a luxury, some non-essential item, the result is exactly the same. We could have saved the life of a child or of many children had we given the money to a famine relief organization like Oxfam America or UNICEF. He notes two differences. One, the child who dies in this example is immediately present and is seen or known by the person who chooses to act selfishly, whereas the children who would be saved by a gift to a relief agency are far away and unknown but nonetheless real. Two, whereas only one child is involved in the case given, a wealthy person could save the lives of many children by giving thousands of dollars that would not ruin the quality of life of the donor. Singer concludes that we are unable to draw a clear moral line between the people in the stories and the rest of us with money we could spare. All the considerations I introduced in the previous section could be repeated. We could argue over whether the long-term problem of hunger is best met by simply giving money to relief organizations or by other efforts that might cost more or less but would be far more effective. I refer to the old principle that it is better to teach people how to fish than to give them a fish. Or we could increase efforts to introduce birth control methods, create better programs of international trade, provide debt relief to poor countries, provide aid to develop better farming methods, sanitation practices, and so on and on. What would be the consequences for the economy and for the solution of other pressing needs, and for many other aspects of society if millions of people suddenly poured huge sums of money into hunger relief? The issues are complicated, difficult, and no easy or obvious answers are forthcoming. But when does making legitimate points become rationalization for our complacency that preserves our comfortable living patterns and whittles down the rigorous demands of *agape* until they become manageable and cost-free? Singer puts his thesis succinctly, "You shouldn't take that cruise, redecorate the house, or buy that pricey suit. After all, a $1,000 suit could save five children's lives." Singer concludes the article by referring to one his examples:

> *When Bob first grasped the dilemma that faced him as he stood by that railroad switch, he must have thought how extraordinarily unlucky he was to be placed in a situation in which he must choose between the life of an innocent child and the sacrifice of most of his savings. But he was not unlucky at all. We are all in that situation.*

The Importance Of The Interpretive Framework: The Role Of Reason And Imagination

The third challenge Christians face today is to move from the principle of love of neighbor that seeks justice for all to their implications for specific issues we face today. It is convenient to speak of the of the application of general principles to particular problems, of theory to practice. However, I suggest that the more fruitful procedure is to begin with the situation and ask how the general ethical perspective provides guidance in making a moral judgment and devising a plan of action.

Creating a universal community in which no neighbor is excluded from consideration and in which each neighbor is held in equal regard with the self would not provide an automatic solution to moral problems. Even if we had an inclusive society in which the rule was from each according to ability and to each according to need, we would still confront thorny problems of justice full of ambiguities, complexities, and quandaries for which there is no perfect solution that benefits all and harms none. Seeking justice for the loved ones requires the use of reason to determine what each is rightfully due. The problems raised by the quest for justice have no simple, obvious rational solution discoverable by all competent reasoners who sincerely seek them. The discernment of the rules according to which social goods are to be justly distributed reflects our historicity and finitude, even when not distorted by selfishness, prejudice, and ignorance. Here it only need be said that we cannot escape the relativity of thought as delineated even when the reasoners are fully in love with the universal community of neighbors for whom they honestly seek justice. Even parents who are totally devoted to their children will not always know infallibly or easily what love requires with respect to each and to all, especially when one child has special needs because of disease, accident, or the presence or lack of talent and ability. In the larger society problems of justice are compounded into conundrums that frequently will have no unambiguous solution even when the best of motives and competent reasoning are presupposed on all sides of the debate. Abortion, affirmative action, policies relating to illegal drugs and prostitution, problems of international trade, and many others illustrate the point. It is easy to get morally indignant about the sweatshops in Asia that produce clothes and shoes cheaply by hiring children and adults at shockingly low wages. American consumers buy them because they cost less than domestically produced goods. Yet it can be cogently argued that without these low-wage jobs, the desperate people there would be even worse off. Having them employed in this way is a defensible, even necessary, first step in a process that will lead them toward eventual prosperity. Yet calling attention to their plight and demanding better conditions for them is also pertinent. Where does realistic reasoning end and self-serving rationalization begin?

It is important at every level to state ethical theory as clearly and systematically as possible. Sloppy thinking leads to inconsistency and confusion about what the principles of action are, how they relate to each other in terms of importance, what their foundations are, when they are to be compromised, and so on. Competing sets of principles differ, and the differences are important. Nevertheless, beyond a point it is not of much value to be so fussy about their purity. Many different ways of stating principles may lead to the same conclusions about what should be done in particular situations. The opposite also holds. Identical general principles may be attached to contradictory views. As politicians say about proposed legislation, "The devil is in the details." So it is with ethics as well. Having high and noble precepts stated eloquently, precisely, and systematically does not guarantee much with respect to their application to specific problems.

It is easy enough to point to some egregious errors of Christians in times past and present who though professing loyalty to biblical norms of love and justice have given support to evil practices in the name of God and the good. Just to take one principle, Christians in every generation have agreed that love is the fulfilling of the law and that love of neighbor is mandated by Scripture. All acknowledge that God requires justice for the poor and oppressed. Scripture plainly says so. Jesus and Paul taught the priority of love, and the Book of Amos is in every Bible. Yet most any destructive and oppressive evil one can name has been supported on Christian grounds by some generation or group of believers. Some obvious examples come to mind: the slavery of Africans, racial segregation, the denial of rights to women, persecution and killing of heretics, the destruction of Native American peoples, their culture, and the theft of their lands, not to mention broken treaties and neglect of their welfare. To this we can add the condemnation of responsible, monogamous same-sex love and the support by Christians of politicians and policies that preserve the prerogatives of the well-off and neglect the have-nots in our society. Christians can be found on every side of disputed moral issues in our time. They read the same Bible and serve the same Jesus, and all profess to honor Christian love and biblical justice. Church members are conservatives, liberals, extremists on the right and left, socialists, capitalists, Democrats, Republicans, and so on. They are all over the place on current ethical problems while acknowledging one faith, one Lord, and one baptism, one God who rules over all.

The explanation of how the same general principles can lead to different positions on specific issues and how different formulations of norms can produce agreement at the level of application lies in the *interpretive framework* operative in the interpreters. Moral imperatives are not simply deduced from generalities when issues are complex. Decisions require interpreters to take into account a variety of considerations not supplied by the high level principles themselves. Obviously the facts and circumstances of the case are crucial. The historical background and the total context in which choice must be made may be essential. If values are in tension — freedom and order, freedom and equality, individual rights and public good, and the like — judgment must be made as to which take priority in just this set of circumstances. Other assumptions enter in as well — the relation of individuals to society, the nature and function of government, the definition of the good life, the good person, and the good society, what human beings need and are capable of achieving morally and otherwise, the source of evil in humanity and the social order, and so on. If biblical texts are employed, they are subject to being variously interpreted, may be qualified or superceded by more primary texts, and so on. Methodological postulates about the ways Scripture, tradition, reason, and experience interact to generate theological and ethical theory figure in. A whole network of interpretive principles, contextual complexities and ambiguities, and the like enter into the determination of what acknowledged moral premises mandate in a specific case.

All of these factors — and others — with which the interpreter works to arrive at a position on particular issues constitute *the interpretive network*. This matrix or framework pertains both to moral norms and to the concrete situation. In every case some interpreter — an individual or a community — puts it all together to unite ethical theory to some specific issue in a given situation with its own peculiar constellation of circumstances. In this way a set of moral judgments is created to form the ethics of belief.

The issue of slavery, about which we all agree today, will make it clear that merely having good principles well stated guarantees practically nothing. Here it is crystal clear that the crucial issues of debate lie not only in the moral norms themselves but also in *the interpretive network*. Prior to the Civil War, Christians were divided between those who wanted to abolish slavery and those who defended it on biblical grounds. Both sides agreed that we should love our neighbors and that God demands justice. The crucial differences lay in how they interpreted the Bible and on some extrabiblical assumptions as illustrated here:

Defenders of Slavery
1. The Bible condones it.
2. Africans are inferior to Europeans.
3. Both races are better off.
4. Natural law justifies slavery. (Aristotle)

Abolitionists
1. Not when rightly interpreted.
2. All are equal in all respects relevant to slavery.
3. Both would be better off free.
4. Natural law supports freedom and equality. (Declaration of Independence)

Or consider a contemporary issue centering around the concept of affirmative action, meaning preferential treatment for groups previously excluded or discriminated against:

Proponents
1. Persons as members of groups.
2. Equality of results.
3. Individual merit may be qualified by other factors: e.g., race and gender.
4. Compensates for past injustice.

Opponents
1. Persons as individuals.
2. Equality of opportunity.
3. Individual merit as sole or primary consideration: Race and gender neutral.
4. Creates new injustices.

Any complex issue could be used to make the point that much goes on between beginning with love and justice from the scriptural side and ending up with a decision about what is morally right in a specific case. While the text, the moral principle, and/or the acknowledged biblical norm may have the first word, many words in between, and next to the last word, the last word is that of the interpreter — and it is the last word that counts decisively. Between love and actual life is the *interpretive framework* that leads the interpreter to make a choice about what love requires in a given situation. Hence, as important and as essential as they are, it is not helpful to get overwrought about the norms themselves. They may not always be decisive or even matter, given what the interpreter does and must do in connecting norms to situation through the medium of a body of assumptions that are not fully resolvable by rational considerations transcendent to all particular points of view.

Moral conversation among Christians who support different social policies would be helped immensely if all parties recognized the important role that the interpretive framework created by human beings plays. Instead in most debates the contending factions proceed as if they are getting their own conclusions straight from the Bible itself. Recognition of the function of an intervening set of assumptions that influences the interpretation of Scripture would help to locate where the crucial issues lie and perhaps facilitate a more fruitful exchange. This is not to deny or disparage the importance of the biblical text itself. It is to say that more is involved. The interpretive framework that mediates the movement from Bible to situation may be the determinative factor and influence what we think the text actually means or implies. Part of the interpretive matrix involves the way we view the Bible itself, its nature, its authority, and especially how we regard the human element in it that reflects the world-view of the biblical authors themselves. The Bible's own highest norms may be adulterated by the cultural relativity of those who wrote it. We have to make a judgment about that. That is why I maintain that in the end we are the functional authority regardless of what our views of biblical inspiration are.

When I function as interpreter the same holds. It is the web of assumptions, preferences, operating procedures, and so on that I bring to the task that determines what positions I will take on specific moral issues. To put it differently, every Christian is a *believer in the church* and a *self in the world*. A great plurality of theological, moral, and social outlooks characterizes our location in the church and in the world. When we ask what Christian norms are, it matters where we are in the church. When we ask what the norms mandate in terms of action, it matters where and who we are in the world — our race, class, region, gender, family, and cultural background, educational level, and so on. It is no wonder that Christians can be found on nearly every side of every moral question. Concrete decision involves always an interaction between these two aspects of our existence. The devil is in the details. My own particular slant is that of an interpreter who is both in the church and in the world who operates within and through the medium of a particular *interpretive matrix*. I can only set forth what I believe.

In Volume II I will illustrate how I move from New Testament norms to contemporary applications of them.

Endnotes

1. For a different perspective on the usefulness of principles, see Stanley Fish, *The Trouble with Principle* (Cambridge: Harvard University Press, 1999). I agree with him that high-level principles cannot be employed to arrive at a rational solution to problems that can be agreed upon by everyone, since their interpretation involves assumptions relative to point of view. Reason is always historically embedded and culturally conditioned. Nevertheless, I believe that an articulation of principles can be useful when understood as part of a system of belief that is acknowledged to be infected with relativity. They can aid in clarifying agreements and differences, even though they cannot be established or refuted by rational considerations thought to be transcendent to relative points of view.

2. My understanding of the human situation is indebted most to Reinhold Niebuhr, *The Nature and Destiny of Man* (New York: Charles Scribner's Sons, 1949), 1:150-300. However, in recent years, my views have increasingly taken markedly different directions from his. He would doubtless fault me for falling into a form of Pelagianism that excessively roots wrongdoing in nature rather than in spirit, in finitude rather than freedom. I in turn am convinced that the existentialism and Augustinianism he represents neglects the grounding of spirit in a biological substratum of energies and impulses that influences though it does not determine the self in its choices. Wrongdoing proceeds from nature and spirit.

3. I acknowledged the validity of the feminist claim that self-exaltation may be the more typical transgression of men, while self-depreciation is more characteristic of women. Numerous questions arise. Gender dissimilarities in moral failure, as well as in ethical reasoning and virtue, may be rooted in biology. Primordially, more similarity is likely between the sexes than is evident in present experience. I am not convinced that women are at heart free from tendencies toward self-glorification when the means to lord it over others are at hand, although men may be more innately inclined toward aggression and violence than women. Neither are men free from self-deprecating tendencies, timidity, and the failure to assert themselves.

4. The preceding paragraphs on sin have been taken from my *The Many Faces of Evil: Reflections on the Sinful, the Tragic, the Demonic, and the Ambiguous* (Lima, OH: CSS Publishing Co., 1997), 73-5. For a fuller development, see 59-78.

5. We can learn much, e.g., from the research of Jean Piaget, Lawrence Kohlberg, Carol Gilligan, and others with respect to how moral character develops in children in a progression toward maturity and the supreme ideals of virtue. See Lawrence Kohlberg, *The Philosophy of Moral Development: Moral Stages and the Idea of Justice* (San Francisco: Harper & Row, 1981), Carol Gilligan, *In a Different Voice: Psychological Theory and Women's Development* (Cambridge: Harvard University Press, 1982), and other works by them and their critics.

6. The point of view developed here has much in common with ideas of Rorty expressed in *Philosophy and Social Hope* (New York: Penguin Books, 1999), 72-90. "So it is best to think of moral progress as a matter of increasing *sensitivity*, increasing responsiveness to the needs of a larger and larger variety of people and things ... as a matter of being able to respond to the needs of ever more inclusive groups of people." 81. Rorty, however, wants ethics without principles. Although we both start with history and operate with a notion of a social self, I believe that principles are not excluded but serve a useful purpose when set within the proper context and their limitations noted.

7. Hence, we may have much to learn from David Hume, *Enquiry Concerning the Principles of Morals* (1751), and Adam Smith, *The Theory of Moral Sentiments* (1759), both influenced by Francis Hutcheson. I agree, then, with Rorty that David Hume with his theory of moral sentiments may be closer to the mark than Immanuel Kant with his notions of subjecting the will to the universal law of reason. Rorty also speaks positively on John Dewey and Annette Baier in this regard. However, my differences from Dewey and Rorty may be even deeper since I set ethics within a religious framework whereas they are secular humanists for whom the human community is the final point of reference. See *Philosophy and Social Hope,* 72-90.

8. This is the memorable way phrase of H. Richard Niebuhr, *The Purpose of the Church and its Ministry* (New York: Harper and Brothers, 1956).

9. One of my college professors said that the first time he heard a white man call a black man brother was not in a church but in a labor union. That remark had a great impact on me as did the reading in college of such books as H. Richard Niebuhr, *The Social Sources of Denominationalism* (New York: Henry Holt and Co., 1929), and Liston Pope, *Millhands and Preachers* (New Haven: Yale University Press, 1942), which laid out in embarrassing detail the extent to which race, class, and other worldly factors were present in denominations and congregations. Both authors later became my teachers at Yale Divinity School.

10. For a recent statement of the view that Jesus was an apocalyptic prophet who thought the world would end in his own lifetime, see Bart D. Ehrman, *Jesus: Apocalyptic Prophet of the New Millennium* (New York: Oxford University Press, 1999).

11. A typical way is to refer to Mark 13:32, where Jesus says no one, not even himself, knows the day or the hour. But that means that no one knows when *within this generation* it will happen, as verse 30 plainly indicates. Of course, one can always say that generation refers to this present age, but that seems unlikely in light of Mark 9:1, 14:62, and Matthew 10:23. Just yesterday (September 9, 1999), I heard a television evangelist say that "this generation" refers to the generation in which all the signs of the end occur. There is no end to the ingenuity that can be exercised to make texts fit the meaning desired or required by the interpreter to save what otherwise would wreck the theory being supported.

12. This is not to deny that the teachings of Jesus can be understood as condemning the oppression of the poor and marginalized. But there is no call for organized resistance to the prevailing social order in the interest of reform anywhere in the New Testament, and it would have been futile to do so in any case. For an impressive interpretation of Jesus as denouncing injustice and preaching good news to the poor, see William R. Herzog, *Jesus, Justice, and the Reign of God* (Louisville: Westminster John Knox Press, 2000), and *Parables as Subversive Speech: Jesus as Pedagogue of the Oppressed* (Louisville: Westminster John Knox Press, 1994).

13. See my *Process Ethics: A Constructive System* (Lewiston, NY: Edwin Mellen Press, 1984), 125-94, 241-50.

14. Alfred North Whitehead, *Adventures of Ideas* (New York: Mentor Books, 1966), 25.

15. See Hans Dieter Betz, *Galatians* (Philadelphia: Fortress Press, 1979), 189-201. Karl Barth says that, of course, there is equality, but there is an order in that equality, whatever that means besides enabling him to have both Galatians 3:28 and sexual hierarchy! Some segregationist ministers in the South a half-century ago argued that love and equality were spiritual matters that had no necessary social and political implications one way or the other.

16. H. Richard Niebuhr in *Christ and Culture* (New York: Harper & Row, 1951) describes five positions Christians have held relating "Christ" and "culture," all of which can claim some New Testament support and have both strengths and weaknesses.

17. Much of the rest of the chapter is a slight revision of material taken from my *Process Ethics*, 174-9.

18. *The New York Times Sunday Magazine* (September 5, 1999), 60-3.

19. Singer indicates that he got this story from Peter K. Unger, *Living High and Letting Die: Our Illusion of Innocence* (New York: Oxford University Press, 1996).

Index Of Persons

Allison, Henry E., 47
Aquinas, 30, 39
Aristotle, 24, 26, 39
Augustine, 39, 161, 177

Barth, Karl, 39, 203
Berlin, Isaiah, 75, 122, 123
Bernstein, Richard J., 103
Brunner, Emil, 39

Calvin, John, 39, 177
Campbell, Will, 136

Davidson, Donald, 74, 82, 103-104
Dewey, John, 89
Dodd, C. H., 139, 140
Dworkin, Ronald, 75

Everill, Brian, 45

Firth, Roderick, 26
Fish, Stanley, 200
Frankena, William, 117-120, 123, 124

Gamwell, Franklin, 30-31, 32
Gewirth, Alan, 29-30, 32

Habermas, Jürgen, 120-122, 124, 125
Hauerwas, Stanley, 39, 163
Herzog, William R., 202
Hume, David, 201

James, William, 85, 100

Jesus, 24, 36, 125, 137-156, 170, 178, 180-182, 196

Kant, Immanuel, 25, 188

Locke, John, 30

Meir, Golda, 173
McClendon, James W., 163

Niebuhr, H. Richard, 13, 39, 128, 202, 203
Niebuhr, Reinhold, 13, 25, 37, 39, 121, 147, 148-151, 156, 184, 189, 200
Nozick, Robert, 29, 32, 124
Nygren, Anders, 147, 158, 160

Peirce, James Sanders, 120
Plato, 39, 46, 78, 79, 89
Pope, Liston, 202

Rachels, James, 114-117, 118, 119, 123
Ramsey, Paul, 147
Rawls, John, 26-29, 32, 120, 124
Ritschl, Albrecht, 126
Rorty, Richard, 62, 73, 77-106, 201

Sadat, Anwar, 173
Schleiermacher, Friedrich, 126
Sellars, Wilfred, 105
Singer, Peter, 192-194
Smith, Adam, 201

Tillich, Paul, 134
Tracy, David, 132

West, Cornell, 37
Whitehead, Alfred North, 13, 62, 89, 157, 184
Williams, Daniel Day, 147

Index of Subjects

abortion, 12
affirmative action, 198
agape, 10, 139, 141-143, 147-153, 174, 182, 184, 186, 191, 192
    and *eros*, 157-163
    See also, love
assisted death, 12

Baptists, 135-136
biblical ethics, 137-147
bio-historical approach, 9-10

capital punishment, 12
categorical imperative, 25
Christianity and civilization, 11, 180-188
church and state, 12
churches, role of, 177-180

Darwinian epistemology, 88
deontological ethics, 30, 31, 38, 164

equality, 12, 24-30, 123-124
eros, 9, 10, 168-170, 174, 179
    and *agape*, 157-163
    See also, love
ethics, 15-48
    and relativism, 70-73
    as beliefs about morality, 16-23
ethics of belief, 7, 8, 13, 16-45
ethics on the boundary, 7, 13
experience, 89-99

feminist theology, 201
foundationalism, 80, 103

fundamentalism, 126
freedom, 12, 26-30, 123-124

God, 9, 20, 25, 30-31, 40, 46, 62, 64, 73, 115-116, 137-147, 170, 181, 186
Golden Rule, 24
grace and law, 190

health care system, 12
homosexuality, 13
hubris, 169

illegal drugs, 12
interpretive framework, 194-200

justice, 7, 10, 11, 12, 24-32, 137-147, 167, 170, 180

law and grace, 190
liberalism, 126
love, 10, 11, 12, 137-163, 168-177, 191, 192
    and civilization, 180-194
    ethical and ecstatic, 153-157
    See also, *agape* and *eros*

moral truth, 107-134
"myth of the Given," 105

natural law, 107-114
neo-orthodoxy, 126

objectivism, 51-52, 53, 67

panpsychist, 74
post-liberal theology, 127

pragmatism, 8, 9, 23, 77-106
    and realism, 99-101
prostitution, 12

realism, 99-101
reason, 32, 107-125
    and imagination, 192, 194-200
relativism, 8, 9, 18, 49-75, 77-106, 112, 113, 116, 118-120, 125
    objective, 52-61, 69, 70-73, 85
    subjective, 53, 54, 67-68, 85
revisionism, 127
revelation, 125-132

sin, 168-170
skepticism, 8, 9, 18-21, 60, 112, 125
slavery, 35, 185, 198
state, 186

teleological ethics, 30-31, 38, 164
truth, 8, 12, 32, 49-76
    correspondence theory of, 61-66
    See also, moral truth

women, status of, 185

www.ingramcontent.com/pod-product-compliance
Lightning Source LLC
Chambersburg PA
CBHW051924160426
43198CB00012B/2023